MW01240733

Still Working While Black

The Untold Stories of Student Affairs Practitioners

A Volume in Identity & Practice in Higher Education-Student Affairs

Series Editors

Pietro A. Sasso
Stephen F. Austin State University
Shelley Price-Williams
University of Northern Iowa

Still Working While Black

The Untold Stories of Student Affairs Practitioners

Editor

Antione D. Tomlin
Anne Arundel Community College

INFORMATION AGE PUBLISHING, INC.
Charlotte, NC • www.infoagepub.com

Library of Congress Cataloging-in-Publication Data

CIP record for this book is available from the Library of Congress
http://www.loc.gov

ISBNs: 979-8-88730-231-7 (Paperback)

979-8-88730-232-4 (Hardcover)

979-8-88730-233-1 (ebook)

CONTENTS

INTRODUCTION

Antione D. Tomlin

Student affairs can be and is a very rewarding profession for many. In the same breath, the profession has not always been kind to Black practitioners. Birthed from a positive response to the first edition of this book, *Working While Black: The Untold Stories of Student Affairs Practitioners*, this text continues the conversation of still working while Black. Additionally, there are more Black voices and stories that need to be told and heard. So, this book provides another space for narratives, lessons, and wisdom to be shared from Black practitioners for Black practitioners. Moreover, this book creates space for Black people to tell their stories, curating insight into what the future of student affairs may look like (Tomlin, 2022).

As revealed in the first edition, I am a recovering student affairs practitioner. While I am no longer directly in student affairs, all of my work is supporting students. I also frequently lean on my training, background, and experience in student affairs to support my students in my courses as a full-time faculty member. Having been a Black student affairs practitioner, I know the joy, happiness, and peace of being a professional in the field. I, too, know the pain, sweat, tears, and challenge that comes with working while Black in student affairs. While the work is not easy, it is necessary. Just as the work is necessary, the praise is too. So, I use this moment to thank the 18 contributing authors who previously paved the way in the first edition of this book. To Jenn, DeShawn, Kisha, Jasmine, DeAnna, Avina, Geoffrey, Corey, Relius, Olajiwon, Laventrice, Davida, Dorothea, Jayson, Zakia, Aja, LaDarius, and Kira, you all did the work to make sure the field heard your untold stories, and I appreciate and thank you for that! Keep being the rockstars that you are!

One of the aims of this book is to continue digging into the untold stories of Black student affairs practitioners. With the complexities and challenges presented to Black practitioners, there is no "ONE" or monolithic Black experience; therefore, another book, this book aids in continuing to build on the literature that speaks to the experiences of Black professionals in student affairs. All Black student affairs voices are essential and even more critical to telling their own stories. The 17 contributing authors in this text share their untold stories for bettering themselves, their students, and higher education. Together, they provide more insight into understanding the experiences of Black student affairs practitioners.

While the stories, lessons, wisdom, and advice provided in each chapter differ, we follow a similar chapter layout. Each author shares their lived experiences while sharing current and previous positions held in the field. Next, chapters explore challenges and opportunities experienced by Black practitioners. Then tips, strategies, and advice for potential and current Black practitioners are provided, along with recommendations for administration and higher education institutions more generally. Last, each chapter ends with words of affirmation to help support their journey in student affairs as Black practitioners. We include these affirmations in hopes that they will add to the support and encourage Black practitioners to make decisions that allow them to practice self-care and make decisions that will keep them safe.

This book explores three themes crafted organically from the opportunities, challenges, advice, and recommendations the authors share in their chapters. The themes used as a foundation for telling the untold stories of this text include (a) "I Said What I SAID: My Voice Matters!," (b) "At the End of the Day, I GOT ME!" and (c) "You Gon' Get Me: ALL of Me!" As mentioned previously, each chapter follows a specific flow and organization. The themes listed serve as a backdrop to a larger conversation that the text is generally entering about the experiences of Black student affairs practitioners. Below, more details of each theme are described.

Theme 1: I Said What I SAID: My Voice Matters!

The practitioners who contribute to this theme stand firm in what they say and their decisions to support themselves and their students. Some voice feeling isolated and contemplating if they made the right decision, questioning their entire existence as a student affairs practitioner. Others share the microaggressions, stereotypes, and biases they have to deal with as professionals in the field. While sharing lessons learned, these Black practitioners share moments in which they step in their voice and stand true and firm to who they are as Black professionals working in student affairs. Ultimately, it is these moments of genuineness and authenticity that allow these Black practitioners to say what they mean, mean what they say, and believe that they, too, matter.

Theme 2: At the End of the Day, I GOT ME!

Practitioners who contributed to this theme focus on self-care while also realizing that they are the ones who will always have their best interests in mind. Many share what seems to be horror stories with silver linings. However, in the end, each author shares the values and importance of being mindful of burnout and its warning signs and effects, as well as the importance of remembering that *YOU* have your best interest at heart. Many of these authors also acknowledge that racism, discrimination, and favoritism are very much alive in student affairs. Hence, as Black practitioners, it is important to stay vigilant and mindful of for whom the space you work was created.

Theme 3: You Gon' Get Me: ALL of Me!

The practitioners in this theme make it known that their Blackness is not to be altered. They acknowledge that they are Black in white space, and they also recognize that their Blackness is an essential part of their core identity, approach, and support to helping students, especially students who look like them. Consequently, the authors share moments that created tension for them as Black practitioners and how they navigated that space. Additionally, they share how stepping into and standing in their Blackness is a value added to the student experience and institution always.

We, as a team, know we have a responsibility to be sure that readers know that the stories you will read and learn from do not represent all Black experiences. So, we encourage you to take each story as an individual picture that adds to a collective collage. Each chapter helps to tell the story, but in no way is the entire story. We further encourage you to explore any reactions, emotions, or feelings that may arise from diving into the pain, hurt, joy, and happiness that is what comes with practitioners who are still working while Black and all the untold stories.

In true tradition, I end this chapter by saying thank you to the 17 contributing authors. They wholeheartedly committed their experiences, hard work, and stories to further the conversation on what it means to be a Black student affairs practitioner. To Kristina, Tasha, Katina, Marcedes, Sarah, Eboni, Jamie, Erica, Dana, Terrell, Nathan, Jamarco, Dyrell, Michelle, Caryn, Ebony, and Andrew, what you SAY matters! AND, I will always create spaces for us to be ALL of us! Thank you for saying yes to this journey and creating space to make our voices heard and stories told. My hope for you all is that you continue to make decisions that support you as you navigate the world and lean into what you are led to do.

REFERENCE

Tomlin, A. D. (Ed.). (2022). *Working while Black: The untold stories of student affairs practitioners*. Information Age Publishing.

SECTION I

I SAID WHAT I SAID: MY VOICE MATTERS!

CHAPTER 1

A COSTLY TALE FROM A BLACK PRACTITIONER

Kristina Collier

Higher education is oftentimes seen as this mechanism for social mobility sorting and sifting students into their "proper" fields. Although social mobility is something many of us seek, higher education has a way of picking and choosing those that are worthy to move up the ladder. When it comes to being Black in these higher education spaces the ladder seems to always be out of order or in the process of being repaired. Black professionals/students are paying a price for achieving higher levels of success and realizing it costs to be the boss and we just so happen to be paying more. Black professionals are routinely pressured to adapt to the standards of institutions built on White supremacy and oftentimes mask their Blackness to do so. This chapter will explore the cost Black professionals/students pay while navigating White spaces, and how we can shift that narrative.

Introduction

As I sit to write this chapter, I can honestly say I never thought I would find a home in the student affairs world. As a current practitioner of higher education, I began my humble beginnings in residential life. I was stumbling and fumbling through what being a live-on professional meant, while also trying to come into my own as a graduate student. Being able to count on one hand all the Black people in my department made it very easy for me to sum up my experiences so far in student affairs and that was siloed.

Still Working While Black:
The Untold Stories of Student Affairs Practitioners, pp. 3–7
Copyright © 2023 by Information Age Publishing
www.infoagepub.com

I was embarking on a journey that was entirely new for me and trying to navigate being a Black professional with no other representation in the classroom or on the job. The pressure to be my best Black self at times had me suffocating and struggling to find a place for myself where I could fit. I felt pressure from myself, pressure from my faculty and department and friends. Pressure to quickly assimilate while still trying to be my authentic self. Nevertheless, I was excited to be embarking on a new journey as a graduate student and balancing an assistantship in residential life but what I did not expect was that I would feel so alone. I also did not expect that I would feel like I was under a microscope with everyone waiting and expecting me to fail. Granted I put a lot of pressure on myself to succeed but never imagined that navigating higher education as a Black woman would be so taxing. The hidden cost of being a Black professional in higher education is you may feel alone. No matter how big my network grew, or how many tables my professors tried to invite me to, they missed the point that I was still Black. I was still the only Black woman at my job and in the classroom, and that feeling of being alone wasn't something I could shake.

My Testimony

Hence, this book chapter isn't just a theoretical summary of what it cost to be Black in higher education but is a memoir and a testament to both my struggles and my successes. This chapter is a reflection of what growing and developing at a predominantly White institution felt like for me and how regardless of the challenges I faced I still graduated and excelled. The cost we pay as Black professionals is oftentimes not spoken about or brushed under the rug, and I for sure wasn't expecting to come into graduate school and feel all of the pressures of being a Black woman, as I had navigated undergrad just fine. In academia, we talk about the hidden curriculum and all the things that aren't shared with incoming graduate students, but we never talk about how it feels to be a marginalized student in academia. There's a cost to moving up the ladder, a cost of trying to fit in, and a cost to not being too Black but not acting too White. There was a cost to being one of the only Black women in my department and that played a major role in my success and failures. I had to learn quickly how to navigate my feelings, while still being professional. Moreover, I had to take the side-eye from my professors while hoping it wasn't because I was Black. I suddenly felt like I wasn't enough, and that I had gotten into my master's program by chance. I never thought to much about imposter syndrome and now it was the only thing taking up space in my mind.

As a Black woman, I had to adjust to how my predominantly White institution functioned. In my work and school spaces, I was never able to fly under the radar and was oftentimes made to feel like the token Black girl for the department helping them to check their box of being diverse. Being the only Black woman in our residential life department and most of my classes wasn't a badge of honor for me. I had to navigate microaggressions and consistently remind my department that saying you value diversity and want to bring a diverse population in means nothing if you don't have the tools to help those marginalized bodies succeed. I was offended by people in leadership on more than one occasion and had to ask myself is it all worth it? Being in a department that didn't celebrate Black History Month and then with police brutality being on the rise against Black people I was being asked to lead sessions and hold forums like I wasn't also suffering. I was putting so much pressure on myself to overperform, overachieve, and overcommit because I didn't want anyone saying the Black girl in the department couldn't hold her own. For me, I felt that if I didn't succeed then it was a reflection of my race and gender. "Oh she's Black, of course she wasn't qualified to do this job," or "of course, she came up short she's a woman." These statements would repeat in the back of my mind and every day I would wake up praying and hoping to never fail. I had countless meetings with my supervisors who never seemed to understand my need to overperform and many of them couldn't even empathize with me. Imagine to my surprise wanting and needing an outlet to express my frustrations and my fears but having no one in my department who even remotely understood what I was going through, and the type of experiences I was enduring as a new graduate student. I not only was trying to maneuver and find my footing in a graduate program that challenged me intellectually but I had to navigate not wanting to quit every day and not giving "them" the satisfaction of saying we knew she wouldn't last. However, as much as that's always the story that sells, the one about my frustrations and my struggles wasn't my truth. The truth is through these struggles and the cost I paid to succeed in higher education at the end of the day I did just that, I succeeded.

Light at the End of the Tunnel

As Black professionals, we oftentimes forget that through all the struggles there is light at the end of the tunnel. As I began to find my way, I realized walking in my Blackness opened a lot of doors for me. I was able to speak to undergraduates about the power of their voice and encourage them to advocate for themselves and others who shared marginalized identities. I was seen as an ally and confidant to many marginalized students who did not share the same identities as me merely because they knew as a Black woman I understood what it felt like to be underrepresented, unheard, and oftentimes unseen. As a Black woman, there were some spaces that I could more easily navigate because of who I was. I was offered diversity roles and helped with recruitment and was oftentimes the face of my department to prove we were inclusive. I struggled with taking some of these roles because I did not want to be seen as the token Black girl but I also had to realize that if I wanted to see a change in my department I had to be more vocal and deal with being uncomfortable if it was for the greater good. I stayed in my department because I didn't want to see anyone else struggle the way I did. In reality, through my struggles, I gained my voice. I began to vocalize how I felt and how many of our marginalized bodies felt inside and outside of the classroom. I made sure that in whatever opportunity I was offered that our learning outcomes centered on diversity and inclusion. My department was nowhere near perfect but I needed to make sure that as long as my Black self was occupying any space I vocalized what I saw and what I felt hindered the department from moving forward.

Unfortunately, the cost we pay as Black professionals in higher education is oftentimes pricey and I have seen phenomenal Black practitioners be burdened by a system that was set up for them to not succeed. I've had too many conversations with Black professionals about how they felt there was no space for them here in higher education and how they couldn't keep trudging through the same systemic racism every day and they shouldn't have to. My advice wasn't to tell them to grin and bear it because for far too long we have done that. I wanted them to find a space where they could be unapologetically themselves and thrive. Through my trials, I've learned that to successfully navigate the student affairs world you have to vocalize your concerns. I realized about a year into my program and my assistantship that I wasn't going to be able to sit and be quiet. I began to challenge my department and question why we had policies and procedures in place that were biased. I began to challenge the microaggressions and call out things that I saw as overtly racist. I figured if my department valued diversity, social justice, and inclusion as much as they say they did then acknowledging their pitfalls wouldn't be a problem. I also began to find allies in my department who truly valued me as a person and wanted to see me succeed. I built a relationship with my leadership team and was able to more comfortably come to them with my issues and the issues I saw in the department. Building a rapport allowed people to see that I was serious about not only advocating for myself but others as well and that I would continuously do so even if no one stood with me. I intentionally tried to find a network of Black practitioners that I could connect with and share our experiences. Realizing I wasn't alone in how I was feeling or being treated validated my experiences and allowed me to see that I wasn't over exaggerating as I was often made to feel. Lastly, I made sure that when the opportunity came to present at forums or when I was asked to present to undergraduates that my presentations were based around social justice and inclusion and that I told my story while also sharing how I overcame my obstacles. I wanted to encourage others that came after me that although the journey would be difficult at times and you will want to quit that there are resources that they can tap into to help them succeed.

My Reflection

As I continue to reflect on my journey and what has gotten me to this moment, I am currently rounding out the first year of my doctoral program. I reflect on how hard it was for me when I first started my student affairs journey. Writing this book chapter brought back all the memories good and bad of my higher education journey and what has gotten me to this point. I remember crying to my partner about not wanting to finish the program and thinking that I made the worst decision of my life becoming a student affairs practitioner. It had gotten so bad that I forgot why this field brought me joy, I could no longer encourage students to carry on or inspire Black undergraduates to continue to want to be faculty or be in higher education. When I got to that moment, I had to reevaluate and look within and the affirmation that continues to drive me and help inspire me is this little quote "What if I fall but my darling what if you fly." I think about all the times I didn't take a chance or that I let people discourage me or dissuade me from pursuing something that would have opened so many doors for me because they saw my potential and didn't want me to be more successful than them. I had to stop letting everyone choose and dictate my future but me. When I came across this quote it was like a lightbulb turned on and it all just made sense. I had to stop being so afraid to fall, offend someone, and step on someone's toes, and when I did that I realized I could fly. Not only did my career soar but I flourished academically. I had this newfound joy for my field and I felt like finally the shackles were released and I wasn't bound by the pressures I had put on myself and that other people had put on me. As a Black student affairs practitioner, there were many times when I made my seat at the table and had to bring my silverware and plate too, but I was fine doing just that. I'm not waiting around anymore for people to invite me, accept my Blackness or appreciate all I have to over offer as a Black body in their White spaces. Through my affirmation, I've created a different table and a different space that now people want to join me, want to help me, and want to network with me. In closing, I want to send you all off with a word of encouragement. Be encouraged as you navigate the student affairs world and never let anyone make you feel unworthy, or unwelcomed. We as Black practitioners are beneficial to our communities, our networks, our institutions, and our students and we should never forget that.

CHAPTER 2

ESCAPE ROOM

Tasha Wilson

ABSTRACT

Black women are painfully reminded of the microaggressions, stereotypes, and biases faced in higher education. In Predominantly White Institutions a systemic weight is placed on the shoulders of Black women, implying that we deny the core of who we are in pursuit of acceptance. It is time to change the narrative. It is time to unlock a series of past cycles to decode the significance of equity and affirmative action. Minimize the pressure to perform and maximize the moment to produce. We are equipped to break barriers, dismantle myths of professional development, and refocus the lens as to what leadership entails. Who we are and what we have to offer are valuable. As multifaceted change agents, we do not have to wear a cape to feel validated. As we show up for ourselves and flex in our brilliance, we recognize that establishing a seat at the table is not the end goal. Creating institutional change and making an imprint for underrepresented groups is the master plan.

Brief Overview of Previous Positions/Careers Held Within Student Affairs

I have worked in various capacities in student affairs that range from residence life, athletics, dean of student life, counseling, diversity, equity, and inclusion. The positions I have held in student affairs were eclectic in nature. I had a brief stint serving in roles at Historically Black Colleges and Universities (HBCU). However, my experiences were primarily at Predominately White Institutions (PWI), both public and private. Mission and

Still Working While Black:
The Untold Stories of Student Affairs Practitioners, pp. 9–14

size played an intricate part in the culture and climate of the institutions I worked for. Hence, some were more bureaucratic than I had anticipated. The complexities of the roles that I have held shaped who I am as a professional. My current position is a full circle moment for me because it is one that I have desired for an immense amount of time. It is a position that is enjoyable and aligns with my purpose and values. For the first time in my life, I am employed with an institution that is supportive of my mental health, overall well-being, and safety. I have a supervisor who is mission oriented and not checklist driven. Finding an employer that prioritizes my mental wellness and having a supervisor who values me as a person was critical for me. Before obtaining my current role, I was previously employed by an institution who dehumanized me. I personally experienced microaggression and race discrimination. My previous supervisor made it clear that it was their intention to bully me and create a hostile environment until it became unbearable. In being the only minority in the office I was given more work than my White counterparts. In their eyes I had two strikes against me, being Black and being a woman. Ultimately, my previous supervisor used their authority to manipulate C-Suite leadership in believing that I was a threat to the department. My peers told me that I should turn a blind eye to the behavior and be grateful that I was employed by a high-performance achieving institution. I felt like I did not have any support. I suffered in silence as to what I experienced daily until I no longer had the capacity, which landed me in urgent care. After running a series of tests, I was diagnosed with vertigo. The doctor confirmed that exhaustion was the root cause of my diagnosis. After being placed on bedrest I knew that it was time for me to shift.

One Word

Shatterproof is the one word that captures the summation of my experience as a student affairs professional. Every opposition and moment of turbulence has sharpened me to become stronger, wiser, and equipped in honoring my brilliance. Not placing my value in the hands of others and recognizing that in authentically loving who I am makes me unbreakable to the demands of systemic racism. I used to convince myself that wearing a cape as a badge of honor would make me feel powerful and more visible in spaces that were not accepting. I believed that to be super I had to overextend myself. I was captivated by perfectionism and external validation. Overcompensation became detrimental to my growth and legitimacy in academia. Creating a falsehood mentality of what being super looked like, caused me to mismanage the load that I was given. The inception of the COVID-19 pandemic uprooted a great awakening within that led me to pivot in my decisions, my boundaries, and how I showed up daily. A cape does not make me significant, my character does. I no longer allowed the opinions of my White counterparts to take precedence in my leadership capabilities. Leadership extends beyond a title or position. Leadership is the action I take to enter every room as myself as a source of inspiration and influence for others. Choosing to be authentic, doing what is purposeful and being courageous in a room full of silence is what makes me a trendsetter.

Challenges

Have you ever been in a room filled with people yet feel as if no one sees you? That is how it is being a Black woman while working in student affairs. Isolation became a quick acquaintance. The vast majority of institutions "see" you, but they do not acknowledge your presence until it becomes beneficial for them. As a member of an underrepresented population in the field of academia, I was either viewed as a threat or a token but not as a human. It is exhausting to be categorized and not genuinely recognized. My identity was suppressed because of my White counterpart's discomfort. Everything that made me who I am was compartmentalized to fit the mold of their hidden agenda. Inadvertently my choice was taken away because of their privilege and sense of entitlement. Being plagued by the concentrated attempt to stifle my desire of acquiring achievement perpetuated a high stress environment. My experiences made me question if pursuing my professional goals was worth the risk.

Every day I am confronted with modern day slavery because of my race and gender. Regardless of accomplishments achieved, my skills and expertise are minimized by my White counterparts due to being prematurely labeled with stereotypes, prejudices, and biases. Being expected to conform by nodding and smiling without uttering a word drives me insane. Reliving the trauma of my personal experiences and what I witness recurrently in the news brings a level of anxiety and overwhelm that is unexplainable. The moment I occupy the same space as my White counterparts not only am I addressed by the wrong name, but I am provoked to see if I would morph into the ABF ("Angry Black Female"). Their discomfort led to their heightened insecurities which escalated toward their approach in antagonizing me. Being harassed, mocked, and tormented just because of my presence, and intimidated by my skin. My passion would be mislabeled as aggressive. My assertiveness would be coined as having an attitude. Surviving Whiteness subconsciously became a running joke. Often synonymously compared as an *escape room*, in which one must join forces with other members of their identifiable group to implement a strategy and examine puzzles that unlock access in solving a problem to foster change. Essentially, escaping oppression and exploring freedom.

Opportunities

The very thing that others despised were the attributes that provided opportunities for me to effectively navigate the realm of student affairs. I took advantage of the resources that were available in order for me to thrive. I sought out local affinity groups and became active in holding voluntary positions. Having affinity groups is a source of participatory engagement to create institutional change. Additionally, I served on a national level on governing boards that focused on elevating voices of underrepresented populations. This catapulted in helping me network with those who were employed by institutions in the surrounding area, as well as nationwide. Through informal conversation, meet ups, and conferences we were able to cultivate and nurture organic connections. Having the foundational premise of understanding for us to relate to one another yet recognizing that who we are extends beyond that. We were able to unpack our feelings, emotions, and thoughts. For several years we sought out validation from our White counterparts in pursuit of acceptance. So, we reveled in the persona of a superwoman at the expense of our emotional wellness and our identity. In coming together and having the necessary candid conversations, we collectively made the definitive choice to no longer allow invisibility and scrutiny to challenge our credibility in our areas of expertise. We channeled our frustrations into strength by going against the grain and courageously did what we were already equipped to do, which is to show up and be present. Unapologetically be us, taking up space in professional areas where we were not always welcomed. The intersectional ties of who we are mattered. It was up to us to disclose truth and hope into the lives of students who mirrored us. Collaboration and communication strengthened productivity in the workplace. Mentorship was vital in transforming my resistance to resilience. Instead of viewing my experiences from a filtered lens, I was able to view them as turning points for me to acknowledge, address, and conquer. In having the right mentors who aligned with my personal vision and mission statement for my life, I was able to advocate for myself.

Tips/Strategies

Never stop learning and never stop growing. Research and familiarize yourself with policies and how they contribute to the work you desire to implement and execute. As a current and potential student affair practitioner, the greatest way to excel and navigate in academia is to remember why you started. Remember the monumental moment that ignited the ammunition within, leading to your decision of wanting to pursue a role in higher education. Be open to having a mentor to guide you and support your career aspirations. Continually give yourself grace. Although you may bend, do not allow the projection of others to cause you to break. What you have to say, give, and offer is valuable to the lives you are meant to impact. Be honest with yourself and understand that you cannot be all things to everyone. Finding balance in your life and being intentional with implementing self-care in your routine contributes to your personal and professional effectiveness. Break the mental health stigma and incorporate time to regularly speak with someone as you encounter various transitions throughout your journey. Emotional wellness will keep you grounded and centered.

Affirmation

As a lover of language, I use various vices of affirmation throughout my daily interactions. I find the affirmations extremely useful in helping me stay within the student affairs profession. One of my favorite quotes is "Never dim the light that shines from within" by Maya Angelou (2015). This affirmation reiterates that my dreams and aspirations are personal. It reminds me that I must find contentment within by embracing my greatness and staying focused on attaining the goals that I desire. As a daily practice, I say the quote aloud while staring at myself in the mirror. I also have the quote as a screensaver on my work computer, so the message serves as a continual reminder. Each morning I listen to the song "Don't Forget Who You Are" by Common (2020). It is a revolutionary song that affirms who I am and validates my abilities to positively change the world. I always feel unstoppable after listening to that song. It gives me the extra razzle dazzle needed for me to unremorsefully show up as my authentic self and demolish any boxes that others try to place me in.

Black Student Affairs Practitioners

Fostering change requires shifting our mindsets from surviving to thriving. Holding space for one another is essential. Creating safe, brave spaces reflective of awareness, application, and action will uncover the importance of promoting racial equity in student affairs. Looking back at what our ancestors have endured and finding meaningful messages in the historical foundation will empower us to jumpstart robust and inclusive workplace cultures. As we embody the value of our voices and unapologetically celebrate Black excellence we will lead with purpose and sustain an impactful legacy that we have worked so hard to obtain. Although our present has not surpassed much from what existed in the past, we must continually remember that not only is there space for us in student affairs, but we also have the creativity and capability to break glass ceilings in changing the outdated narrative.

REFERENCES

Angelou, M. (2015). *The Complete Poetry*. Random House.
Common. (2020). Don't forget who you are [Song]. On *A beautiful revolution Pt. 1*. Loma Vista Recordings.

CHAPTER 3

LESSONS LEARNED FROM MY SISTER CIRCLE

Katina Moten

ABSTRACT

Compared to other women and Black men, as a Black woman leader I have faced harder to penetrate barriers advancing into leadership and have experienced additional challenges while serving as a leader. However, despite the challenges that I have faced, I have been a successful leader because of the support that I received from my Sister Circle. This group of Black women have had my back, have uplifted me, and have amplified my voice when others have presumed my incompetence, ascribed negative attributes to me, and have invited me to the table, but silenced my voice. This chapter shares my experiences leading as a Black woman at a predominantly White institution (PWI) and highlights the lessons that I learned from my Sister Circle: work in excellence, be authentic, pursue education, pay it forward, and know your worth. These lessons have been invaluable to my success as a leader; therefore, this chapter also reflects my gratitude to my Sister Circle for being a safe space, a support system, and a community of women who have understood me.

WHERE THE JOURNEY BEGINS

Look to your left, look to your right, one of you will not be sitting here at the end of this semester—this was the welcoming message I received in a STEM course. As an undergraduate, traditional-aged college student, I

Still Working While Black:
The Untold Stories of Student Affairs Practitioners, pp. 15–24
Copyright © 2023 by Information Age Publishing
www.infoagepub.com

struggled, as many do, with the initial transition of high school to college. However, as a Black woman pursuing a biology major on a PWI campus, I experienced constant feelings of, "I should not be here, why am I here, I am not good enough"—feelings that magnified my transition issues. Further contributing to my feelings of inadequacy, I rarely found support and encouragement from my White peers who were also pursuing the biology major; and unfortunately, I was uncomfortable speaking with the STEM course instructors, as none of them looked like me and none of them ever made me feel welcomed to reach out and get help. On those rare occasions that I did seek help from my instructors, my interactions with them led me to believing that they did not believe in me nor wanted to see me succeed. Nonetheless, I journeyed through my undergraduate years the best way I knew how: working hard. However, working hard while simultaneously approaching your academics ineffectively does not equate to being the best version of yourself. Regardless of my lack of understanding of how to be a good student and working hard but using my less than desirable approach, I persisted and earned grades that kept me in good academic standing.

Lacking the awareness on how to effectively approach my academics was a significant challenge impeding my success as a biology major. Adding to my challenges was becoming pregnant in sophomore year and having a son at the age of 20. Despite this challenge during sophomore year, I persisted and remained a full-time student throughout my pregnancy, gave birth, and immediately returned as a full-time student. Even with the support of family and friends, the return to full-time studies was hard and I was not confident that I would make it to graduation. Further impacting my confidence, during my junior year, my assigned advisor informed me that my career goals were unrealistic. He said, I should change direction because he could not see me being successful. Upon hearing his words, I felt defeated, and I felt lost. But do you know what, I persisted. I continued completing every course and I tackled everything sent to discourage me, to get me to quit. I persisted to graduation, and I earned my biology degree. I not only earned a bachelor's degree in biology, but I continued my education several years later and I earned a master's degree in leadership and liberal studies. And as the icing on my educational cake, just a few years ago, while working full-time, I completed a doctoral degree in higher education administration. I persisted!

After earning my bachelor's degree, I worked in several positions within higher education and in less than ten years after earning my bachelor's degree, I journeyed into academic advising. I had not set out for an academic advising role; however, when I read the advertisement for the open position and I recalled the experiences I had in my undergraduate years, particularly, the lack of support from my academic adviser, I decided to apply. Those interactions with my undergraduate advisor had stuck with me more than I realized. As I submitted my application materials and participated in the interviews, I promised myself that if hired, I would commit to helping students and would prevent students from experiencing what I had experienced as an undergraduate. The PWI hired me for the position of senior academic advisor for first- and second-year undergraduate students pursuing STEM majors. I was excited to work in this role, and within no time, I was making good on my promise of ensuring that I appropriately encouraged and supported my advisees fully. Also, given my undergraduate experiences and given that this position was on a PWI campus, I paid special attention to minoritized populations, as I did not want them to face the same obstacles I faced when completing my degree, especially the feeling that their advisor does not believe in them. I made sure these students felt welcomed, knew they belonged, and were aware of and used all the resources available to them. For example, I remember when a young Black woman came into my office for an advising appointment to discuss her current semester grades. It was around the midpoint of the semester, and she told me that she was struggling in her chemistry course, not failing, but not earning the grades she wanted to earn. Given her performance in this course, she commented that she was starting to question if she wanted to continue with the STEM major pathway. In response, I reminded her of the long-term goal she had set for herself—going to medical school after earning a biochemistry degree. Additionally, I remember stressing to her that the struggles she faced in the chemistry course were a hurdle, but not a hurdle that was going to end her academic race. Furthermore, I told her she would get through the course and that she was going to accomplish her goal of becoming a doctor. And you know what, she passed that chemistry course and persisted to graduation! Moreover, when other students talked with me about their academic challenges, I took time to ask what they had going on in their life that might be impacting their academic performance. If a student communicated challenges such as struggling with time management, having insufficient funds to purchase course materials, and dealing with roommate issues, I explained the campus resources available to support them, and often, I not only talked about the resources—Learning Center, Financial Aid, Counseling Services—but I walked to these offices with the student or called the offices while the student was in my office to ensure the student got connected to the staff who could help them.

In my first few years as an advisor on the campus, things went well, and I felt as though I was having an impact, helping students, and making connections. My professional life was good, and I enjoyed being an advisor. Then one day, my supervisor alerted me that she received a job opportunity that she could not refuse to accept. She resigned from the director position, and while I enjoyed being an advisor, I decided to apply for the director position. After enduring a nerve-wrecking but fair interview process, the campus leadership hired me to fill the vacancy. I demonstrated I was the best applicant for the position. So, within a span of only a few years, I went from working as an academic advisor to serving as the director of the unit. I was excited, yet hesitant, functioning in my new leadership position. However, my excitement was short-lived, and my hesitancy increased, as I quickly started facing challenges in this leadership role that I had not experienced while serving as an academic advisor.

DEFINING SISTER CIRCLE

Before continuing with my journey, it is essential to briefly discuss how women traditionally experience leadership. It is known by most that women face many challenges ascending into and serving in leadership roles. Helping to explicate this plight of women advancing into leadership is the glass ceiling metaphor. This metaphor highlights how subtle and often invisible barriers negatively affect the experiences of women pursuing and holding leadership roles (Beckwith et al., 2016). Although the glass ceiling explains the plight for women; this metaphor is somewhat inadequate in explaining the additional barriers and challenges that Black women face. Therefore, explicating the unique experiences of Black women leaders is the concrete ceiling metaphor. This metaphor illuminates how Black women, compared to other women and Black men, face harder to penetrate barriers advancing into leadership and experience added challenges while serving as a leader (Barnes, 2017; Beckwith et al., 2016).

Despite the challenges and barriers faced by Black women, many of us are successful in our leadership roles. This success can stem from the lessons we learned through our upbringing, our educational experiences, and our spiritual practices. Similarly, for Black women leading on college campuses, some of us can attribute our success to our access to and use of formal support structures designed to help all staff develop leadership skills (i.e., staff mentoring programs). However, while our institutions provide these leadership development opportunities for us, another source of support (and the one I posit as the most critical for Black women leading on a PWI campus) is a Sister Circle.

According to West (2018), there is value for Black women to come together in a confidential and safe space to share stories of their experiences with microaggressions and have that space to offer insights and advice with each other on how to manage these challenges. Particularly, for Black women at PWIs, these groups are necessary, as there are few opportunities to have connections and support among the Black women student affairs professionals (West, 2019). Spates et al. (2020) corroborates West's assertions by suggesting that Black women can find coping strategies for dealing with gendered racism through being associated and connected to each other. These authors contend that "Within these spaces, Black women are allowed to be themselves and participate in safe discourse that has been essential to their means of survival" (Spates et al., 2020, p. 521). While Spates et al. and West do not specifically use the terminology "Sister Circle" in their research, their observations on how Black women can support one another aligns with the utilization of the sister circle terminology included in the research of Neal-Barnett et al. (2011) on anxiety treatment with African American women. Neal-Barnett et al. state that a sister circle can offer support to Black women with anxiety disorders. These authors also state, "a sister circle is a support group that builds upon existing friendships, fictive kin networks, and the sense of community found among African American females" (p. 266). Considering the research of Spates et al., and West that illuminates how a group of Black women can support each other to cope with challenges and given the definition of a sister circle used by Neal-Barnett et al., for the purposes of this chapter, I define a Sister Circle as a group of Black women working together on the same PWI campus who share common experiences and render guidance, support, and friendship to one another to cope with and thrive in their professional environment. Furthermore, within this definition, I define members of the Sister Circle, as sister friends.

LESSONS LEARNED

Thankfully, when I transitioned into a leadership position to serve as a director on a PWI campus, I had sister friends who supported me. I had the right women surrounding me, women who understood my experiences, women who wanted to see me succeed, and women who pushed me to be my best. This group of Black women were critical to my success, and I learned many lessons from their advice, mental and emotional support, and friendship. Specifically, through engaging in countless conversations; or conversing at breakfast, lunch, and dinner; or talking while taking walks on campus; or chatting on our way to or returning from meetings, my Sister Circle taught me five distinct lessons: work in excellence; be authentic; pursue education; pay it forward; and know your worth.

Work in Excellence

I recall one day, when one of my sister friends told me that a campus colleague (a White woman) was spreading false information about me.

According to my sister friend, this colleague shared with her that my team of advisors was giving inaccurate information to incoming students. This colleague had suggested to my sister friend that she did not think I was aware of how to best serve students so I was not a good hire for the advising center and should not be the one responsible for leading orientation programming for the campus. As my sister friend shared this information with me, I felt myself getting hot. Infuriated, but calmly, I asked my sister friend, what was your response upon hearing all of this. I remember my sister friend telling me that she informed this colleague that the advising team was doing great work and to her knowledge was not giving out bad advice to students. She also mentioned that she told the colleague she was hearing good things from students, parents, and other staff about the advising unit and its leader.

After my sister friend shared with me what happened, I expressed my frustration on how that colleague misspoke not only about my team but also on my leadership skills. I remember wanting to know from my sister friend her thoughts on why the colleague shared what she did with her. My sister friend started out her response by telling me to please trust and believe that I was doing excellent work. She continued, it is important for you to understand, given who we are, our identity, certain people will believe you should not lead. From this conversation with my sister friend, I took away the following lesson:

> People do not want to see you succeed nor do they even believe you will succeed. Individuals will presume you are incompetent and find fault in what you do, even if there is no true fault present. While it is not fair, it is what happens. Therefore, your recourse, our recourse, is to speak up for ourselves and for each other. But more importantly, we must let our actions speak for us. Do the work. Give your best, grind hard, and function within your work in excellence. You do not need to aim for perfection, but you must always strive for excellence. With your excellent work, in time, those trying to defame you will be unsuccessful. People will see your excellent work and will disregard the negative messages because those messages will be inconsistent with the excellent work that they have seen firsthand from you.

Be Authentic

Being a Black woman on a PWI campus, others tend to perceive your confidence and strength for being "mean," "unapproachable," and "cold." Early in my leadership journey, I started to become aware of these perceptions and found myself trying to counteract how others perceived me by being "overly nice," "always smiling," and "being overaccommodating."

While my behavior was having the intended effect—others feeling less intimidated—I felt fraudulent.

There was an evening that I was out to dinner with a sister friend, and as we typically do, we shared how things were going and what was happening at the job. During our conversation, I remember asking my sister friend how she thought others perceived her. To my surprise, she mentioned similar perceptions that others had ascribed to me. One that she mentioned, and it took me by complete surprise was hearing her say how others thought she was unapproachable—as this was the furthest thing from the truth. As we continued in our conversation and sharing our feelings, we were helping each other to think about the perceptions that others held and comforted each other by verbalizing that the perceptions that others held of us were false perceptions. In this conversation we discussed how as Black women leaders, when we set expectations, hold people accountable, be direct, and get the job done, people become intimidated and perceive meanness, coldness, inapproachability from our reasonable and acceptable behavior as a leader. We felt that people's perceptions and intimidation are not about us. From our dinner that evening, the conversation helped me to learn:

> While it can be hard, as a Black woman leader, we can remain confident and continue holding people to high, but realistic standards. Furthermore, it is not problematic if you are not always warm and fuzzy while leading. There is no requirement to function in leadership in that manner. Also, engage in self-reflection. To self-assess and think about how you come across and if in fact, there is room to improve your actions, then yes, do so. But, when adjusting your actions, you must remain authentic. Engage in trainings that help improve your emotional intelligence so you can do your part to be a good leader. And after you have done all that you can for yourself, you can feel comfortable rejecting the labels others try to place on you. Instead, as my sister friends stressed: you can be who you need to be and want to be as a leader and do so authentically.

Pursue Education

Working as a Black woman leader on a PWI campus can mean that others will not hear or recognize your contributions in the way you want. I realized this phenomenon firsthand while serving as a director. Given the position I held, I attended high-level director meetings (so I was at the table). I assumed my presence at these meetings was to meaningfully contribute. However, in many of these meetings, others barely heard my voice. I felt visibly, invisible. In most of these meetings, I was usually the only Black or one of a few. There were many instances in which I would share my comments and give informed opinions to only have those comments unacknowledged. Or, in some cases, the ideas that I shared would be coopted by others who would then implement successful programs based off my ideas and insights; and barely, if at all, acknowledge my contributions in their success. While I would like to be the exception to the rule, my sister friends shared their countless stories of previously having their voices silenced and ideas stolen which corroborated my experiences. In sharing my struggles with my sister friends, of making it to the table, but not feeling heard or recognized, they taught me the following:

> Your experience will get you to the table, but your credentials will help to amplify your voice. Once you earn an advanced degree, those credentials will leverage your experiences and remove another barrier that those in the majority (both men and women with higher degrees) have placed in front of you. If you have the resources and the capacity to do so, earn your doctoral degree. Earning your doctoral degree will not solve everything, but it can help. It can help you to stop feeling visibly, invisible. It can help you to be at the table and to have your contributions heard, supported, and appropriately acknowledged.

Pay It Forward

As I was learning my lessons from the Sister Circle, I was becoming more confident in my leadership abilities. I grew stronger and more comfortable within my position and with this confidence, I started to believe that I was indeed being successful. Once I believed in my success, I knew it was time to expand my Sister Circle and bring in younger Black women professionals. I had this awareness for my obligation to help younger Black women because several of my sister friends always commented, when you have "made it," bring up the younger Black women on campus who are emerging as leaders. These sister friends impressed upon me the following:

[Extract] When you can, you reach back and pull up another woman. You pay it forward; and in doing so, you are helping to ensure the next group of Black women have a roadmap and can use this roadmap to avoid unnecessary challenges. Similarly, when you pay it forward, you have a responsibility to pour into the cups of others. You use your words to build the younger leaders up and not tear them down. You do not turn away an opportunity to mentor other Black women who reach out for mentoring. Additionally, be the voice of the younger Black women leaders when you are occupying spaces that they are not; amplify the voice of younger Black women in those rooms where they are present, but others want to keep them silenced. Moreover, as you walk through doors, you keep them open and help other Black women enter leadership spaces. Bottom line, if you can help, do it. Pull up Black women, as it is an obligation that we should happily and always pay.

Know Your Worth

As I continued my tenure as a leader, I was discovering that when you are engaged in work that you find enjoyable and you believe you are making a difference, then it can be easy to give your all while not getting adequate and necessary support in return. Furthermore, I was recognizing how easy it is to give your best, do increasingly more, and have others constantly taking and not giving back to you. As I excelled in my work and demonstrated my abilities to lead high-performing teams, I had more work added onto my plate of responsibilities. While the additional workload benefitted me, I gained new knowledge and new skills, I paid the price for my competency. My workload had become heavy, and I was exhausted.

While I loved what I was doing, my sister friends pointed out, you have overextended yourself, others are asking you to do too much. And always having my back, my Sister Circle further called attention to the harmful effects of my increasing workload. My sister friends strongly advised me to start saying no and to stop allowing others to take advantage of me. My Sister Circle not only verbalized this lesson for me, but they also demonstrated it, as a few within the Sister Circle who experienced others taking them for granted and professionally abusing them made changes for themselves—they left the institution. These women knew it was time to move on. They secured new positions that better aligned with their professional goals and entered spaces that better supported them as Black women leaders. In hearing the words of my sister friends and observing their behaviors, my Sister Circle taught me:

> You stay where others want you, value you, and support you; when these things no longer exist, then you seek better opportunities and move onto the next position. Moreover, know when enough is enough. Moving on is not quitting, it is protecting your peace and knowing your worth.

FINAL THOUGHTS

Along my journey, my Sister Circle offered me support, advice, and wisdom. The Sister Circle taught me to work in excellence, be authentic, pursue education, pay it forward, and know your worth. I am forever thankful for this group of women, and therefore want to use these concluding thoughts to extend my sincere gratitude to my Sister Circle for allowing me to be me and to make mistakes; engaging in conversations that I was able to laugh and cry; and spending time letting me vent and encouraging me to dream. Because of my Sister Circle, I was able to be me, my full authentic self, and develop into a successful leader on the campus. Like many Black women leaders, despite the challenges faced while leading on the campus of a PWI, I persisted in my role and succeeded with the support of some remarkable women—My Sister Circle!

REFERENCES

Barnes, J. (2017). Climbing the stairs to leadership. Reflections on moving beyond the stained-glass ceiling. *Journal of Leadership Studies, 10*(4), 47– 53.

Beckwith, A. L., Carter, D. R., & Peters, T. (2016). The underrepresentation of African American women in executive leadership: What's getting in the way? *Journal of Business Studies Quarterly, 7*(4), 115–134.

Neal-Barnett, A., Stadulis, R., Murray, M., Payne, M. R., Thomas, A., & Salley, B. B. (2011). Sister circles as a culturally relevant intervention for anxious Black women. *Clinical Psychology, 18*(3), 266–273.

Spates, K., Evans, N. T. M., Watts, B. C., Abubakar, N., & James, T. (2020). Keeping ourselves sane: A qualitative exploration of Black women's coping strategies for gendered racism. *Sex Roles, 82*(9), 513–524.

West, N. M. (2019). In the company of my sister-colleagues: Professional counter-spaces for African American women student affairs administrators. *Gender and Education, 31*(4), 543–559.

CHAPTER 4

DO NOT CALL ME MISS

The Intersection of Gender and Race on the Honorific Title Doctor

Marcedes Butler

ABSTRACT

Suppose you earn a doctorate. You deserve to be respected and called by your title, Doctor. I share my lived experience from the critical race theory lens, utilizing storytelling to make meaning of transitioning from Miss to Doctor as a Black woman administrator in higher education. There are plenty of instances of ambiguity and ways in which gender, race, and civility impact my trajectory in academia. For example, White staff members address me by my first name in emails that address their White colleagues as Doctors. Given the media coverage of journalists dropping "Doctor" from First Lady Jill Biden's name and the 2021 firing of the White official from North Carolina for refusing to use the earned prefix "Doctor" to address Black women, it is the right time to share my experience with the intersections of gender, race, and civility centered on that honorific. This chapter provides recommendations on creating opportunities for change and respectfully demanding to be addressed by one's earned title among current and potential Black student affairs practitioners pursuing doctorates.

INTRODUCTION

This chapter aims to share my lived experience transitioning from "Miss" to "Doctor" as a Black woman higher education administrator. I will share

Still Working While Black:
The Untold Stories of Student Affairs Practitioners, pp. 25–36
Copyright © 2023 by Information Age Publishing
www.infoagepub.com

recommendations on navigating the intersections of gender, race, and civility centered on the honorific title/prefix with current and potential Black higher education practitioners pursuing doctorates. The contradiction between achievement ideology and the social inequities created by race, gender, and social class is a critical issue confronting African American women administrators (Lloyd-Jones, 2009). Accordingly, we need to strengthen our understanding of what African American women in administrative positions experience when working while Black (Lloyd-Jones, 2009). The theoretical methodology that best allows my words to make a difference is storytelling, a significant tenet of critical race theory (CRT) used to elevate minority voices, perspectives, and experiences. Thus, CRT speaks from a critical race-gendered epistemology and focuses theoretical attention on issues of social inequity and injustice (Crenshaw, 1995). This theory allows my narratives to rise and challenge the traditional narratives that shape our society and recognize silenced voices in qualitative data. Furthermore, Solórzano and Yosso's (2002) research on CRT supports my goal of sharing my experiences as a Black woman working in higher education because those injured by racism and other forms of oppression discover they are not alone in their marginality and use the information to become empowered and learn to make arguments to defend themselves. In this sense, storytelling can help promote social justice and civility by putting a human face to the experiences of Black student affairs practitioners.

This chapter will share my lived experience transitioning from "Miss" to "Doctor" as a Black woman higher education administrator to qualitatively address the dominant cultural lack of understanding about the intersectionality of gender, race, civility, and decisions to address minority individuals by their earned titles/prefixes in professional settings. In addition, I will provide an overview of my academic and professional work experiences, a discussion on race and gender, tips and strategies for student affairs professionals to create change, and respectfully demand to be addressed by the earned title/prefix "Doctor" among current and potential practitioners pursuing doctorate degrees. Lastly, I will share the affirmation I use throughout my daily interactions to stay motivated in my profession and conclude with a summary. The terms "Black" and "African American" will be used interchangeably throughout the chapter to describe administrators, practitioners, and professionals.

ACADEMIC AND CAREER PATHWAY

My name is Dr. Marcedes Butler, and I started college in 2001; it feels like I never left because I have remained as a student or employee. I was a full-time college student from 2001 to 2016 and 2020 to 2021. I earned two bachelor's degrees in psychology and Black studies, two graduate certificates in community college-teaching faculty and nonprofit management, a Master of Science in counseling, student development in higher education, and a Doctor of Education (EdD) in educational leadership. One of my professional development best practices is earning a degree at the institution where I am employed.

My area of expertise is academic advising and creating affirmative, structured, and inclusive environments that help students persist to graduation. The research I write and present focuses on the impact of educational and social involvement on degree completion and at-risk student populations. I have worked at proprietary, predominantly White, Hispanic-serving, and minority-serving public and private 4-year institutions with titles such as adjunct faculty, lead retention counselor, assistant director of student services, and director of student success and advising. In 2022, I won the National Academic Advising Association (NACADA) Region 9 Excellence in Advising—Advising Administrator Certificate of Merit for my success with MGM International Resorts and the Nevada System of Higher Education (NSHE) partnership to offer the College Opportunity Program (COP) to MGM International Resorts employees. The COP covers MGM employees' tuition for fully approved online programs at participating NSHE campuses. As of 2019, I am the learning concierge for COP participants at the University of Nevada, Las Vegas. I advise and teach undergraduate and graduate working adults the necessary steps to persist to graduation.

"Persistence" describes my experience as a student affairs professional. When I began my educational journey, I was not confident I would graduate. Still, thanks to compassionate advisors, faculty, and administrators, I completed and surpassed what I thought was the highest level of education I could achieve. I became an administrator who continues to pay it forward. My professional and educational journey is an example of Merriam-Webster's (n.d.) definition of persistent: "existing for a long or longer than usual time or continuously" (para. 1). I beat the odds as a Black woman by persisting through the dissertation and earning a doctorate when doctoral students' attrition or drop-out rate is 50% (Lovitts, 2002). Research by the National Center for Science and Engineering Statistics (2021) confirms the statistics have not changed compared to all other degrees; the doctoral studies completion rate is stagnant at 50%.

Furthermore, the National Science Foundation Annual Survey of Earned Doctorates shows that U.S. universities conferred 55,283 doctorates in 2020; Black students earned 3,095 (National Center for Science and Engineering Statistics, 2021). After working full-time while attending school for over a decade, I did not expect blatant disrespect from my higher education colleagues regarding my updated title/prefix. I thought I was alone in my experience, but this is a common issue among people of color, especially women, regardless of socioeconomic status. For instance, Dr. Jill

Biden, the First Lady of the United States, and wife of the 46th president, was disrespected in front of the world when the media intentionally did not address her as "Doctor." Her treatment is a reminder that women continue to fight for respect irrespective of race.

Throughout my career in higher education, I learned the importance of degree completion for social capital and mobility, so I worked hard to be an example to students by persisting to graduation even when I wanted to give up. I was socialized to think that obtaining a college degree and working hard would bring respect and open doors to opportunities, but that changed when I earned my doctorate. Immediately after graduation, my prefix changed, and so did my racialized experience. Compulsorily, I internalized that being one step ahead, outworking others, and maintaining a consistent track record of student success did not automatically earn the respect of being called Dr. Butler on college campuses. The fight for equity and inclusion is an ongoing epidemic for Black higher scholar-practitioners. The racial disparities, emotional tolls, and invisible burdens within academia are so harmful that they have caused scholars to use their experiences working while black as a call for help (Butler & Whitehead, 2021; Conerly & Butler, 2020; Tomlin, 2022).

I often questioned how employees of a higher education institution that promotes social justice, inclusiveness, and respect could be insensitive. In 2021, I coauthored an article on the impact of mentorship and sponsorship on Black women administrators (Butler & Whitehead, 2021). I told a story of a powerful White administrator without a doctorate who advocated for me and addressed me as Dr. Butler in formal emails to the executive leadership teams. A White male demanding his counterparts respect me increased my reputation among senior leaders and forced them to address me by my title in professional settings (Butler & Whitehead, 2021). As Black students and affairs professionals, we can model that energy by demanding respect for each other and sharing the steps, requirements, and experience needed to move along this unknown, unchartered pathway for higher education administrators (Butler & Whitehead, 2021).

It was shocking and hurtful to experienced professionals diligently not address me as Dr. Butler, especially when interacting with students. It has been over five years since I earned my EdD from the University of Southern California (USC), and it became evident that using incorrect personal pronouns is more offensive than not addressing someone by their earned title/prefix.

RACE AND GENDER

The following section will discuss the impact of race and gender on the challenges and opportunities I experience as a student affairs professional.

Professional Organizations

Research reveals that African American female administrators encounter significant academic barriers that discourage them from becoming "productive and satisfied members" (Turner et al., 1999, p. 28). I agree because the feeling that I am not worthy of being called "Doctor" on college campuses and professional organizations has caused isolation, loneliness, and lack of trust that interfere with my full participation in academia (Esnard & Cobb-Roberts, 2018; Patton, 2009; Tomlin, 2022). Like most scholar-practitioners, I am a member of several professional organizations that support my academic, career, and social goals. I noticed on one such organization's website that some names were missing the title "Doctor." I assumed this was a clerical error and that the organization's staff would correct the prefixes immediately. However, I received a disheartening and disrespectful response stating that they removed "Doctor" from all the names listed. I thought, "Wow, this organization is a direct reflection of my passion, and they dismissed me!" In full transparency, that action hurt my feelings since the executive director was a woman of color with a doctorate. After that interaction, my participation declined, and I did not renew my membership. This is another example of how the fight against systemic racism is a corrosive and widespread problem in our culture, and we all need to confront it better.

Challenges

I am no stranger to the upheaval that Black women face in academia. I choose to share my story as a Black doctoral student and Black woman administrator so that the intended audience gains a greater sense of my truth because my words and actions are presented as they are intended (Conerly & Butler, 2020). It was not until my title/prefix changed from Miss to Doctor that I exclusively experienced macroaggressions and macroaggressions from individuals at institutions that promote degree completion. The two examples I share below happened years ago. Still, as a Black woman who disseminates information required to accelerate success, I must convey my experiences breaking down barriers preventing Black administrators from academic and career mobility (Butler & Whitehead, 2021).

Emails: There are two categories of doctorate degrees: academic and professional. Academic degrees, such as the PhD, focus on research, data analysis, and theory evaluation. A professional doctorate, such as an EdD, is intended for practitioners seeking to apply their knowledge to practice in educational leadership roles. I know the difference, and so do my colleagues, but I understand that students might not be privy to abbreviations' differences. Hence, in my email signature, I list my name as "Dr. Marcedes

Butler" instead of "Marcedes Butler, EdD" In addition, I clarified who I am and how I want to be addressed in a professional setting.

Most students and colleagues call me Dr. Butler, but others weaponized my race and gender by intentionally not calling me by my title. I am Dr. Butler; do not call me Miss! For example, when I worked at a university classified by Carnegie as an R1, or Very High Research, institution, two White women staff members addressed me by my first name in emails to students. They mentioned their White colleagues by the title "Doctor." If the staff members know that I have a doctorate, and my email signature lists it, what other reasons besides race, gender, and age would cause some-one in academia to be disrespectful? These staff members taught students to continue negative, discourteous behavior ingrained in systematic racism. Students followed the example and addressed me by first name or Miss in their responses. After repeating positive affirmations or saying a prayer, I straightaway corrected the students and colleagues regarding how to address me. The fact that I have to fight to be called by my earned title is another example of racism that is alive and well. Training on diversity, equity, and inclusion aims to reduce and prevent stereotyping and uncon-scious bias, but I have not experienced a change on college campuses. The act of selecting who receives power, prestige, and respect is an example of overt discrimination I experienced when working while Black in student affairs.

Publication: The rules of written communication are often governed by the Associated Press (AP) stylebook, which outlines English grammar, usage, and style. In an opinion piece, Elizabeth Jensen, NPR's public edi-tor, explained how NPR and many other publications apply the stylebook's standards when referring to doctors and PhD holders (Advisory Board, 2018). Jensen wrote, "Longstanding NPR policy," based on criteria cards in the AP stylebook, "is to reserve the title of 'Dr.' for an individual who holds a doctor of dental surgery, medicine, optometry, osteopathic medi-cine, podiatric medicine, or veterinary medicine." Jensen noted that the AP further clarifies, "If appropriate in the context, Dr. also may be used on the first reference before the names of individuals who hold other doctoral degrees (Advisory Board, 2018, para. 4).

I was unaware of the AP stylebook when I reviewed an article for which I provided quotes on a campus initiative. My recommended edits included updating my title to "Dr. Butler," but my request was denied due to the AP stylebook's rules. I was told that "Doctor" is used for medical doc-tors only. I was in disbelief that the article ran without the correct prefix or any acknowledgment that I earned a doctorate, especially in a pub-lication centered on higher education. Mrs. Michelle Obama, the first African American first lady of the United States, specified, "After decades of work, we (women) are forced to prove ourselves again." I agree with Mrs.

Obama's statement. I grew resentful for spending over a decade in school earning the highest degree and still not receiving the respect I deserve. After that experience, I took notice of written publications and found that, more often than not, "Doctor" was used regardless of the type of doctorate. I also noticed that the rules depend on the author or editor's discernment of the AP stylebook. The insult was unintentional, but I felt disrespected regardless of the intent. A lack of respect in written publications is another example of Black student affairs professionals' issues.

Opportunities

My experience working while Black in student affairs has been primarily positive because my roles directly impact student success and graduation. I get joy from helping students persist to graduation; thus, the good experiences outweigh the bad. Being a Black woman is a great experience full of opportunities. We are known to get things done and are expected to succeed even in the most challenging situations. Being socialized that Black women are powerful and can do it all helped me expand my academic and professional experiences in student affairs because I did not know any better. According to Gregory (2001), Jean-Marie and Brooks (2011), and Henry and Glenn (2009), Black women have demonstrated a great deal of resiliency despite being hidden behind the tripartite-layered veil of persecution due to their race, gender, and class. Cocreating the student organization JENGA is one of the many opportunities my race and gender gave me along my career pathway.

JENGA: At USC, I cofounded JENGA Doctoral Association (JDA), a peer support group with seven other Black women in our doctoral program. The official JENGA name has roots in the Swahili language and West African principles of wisdom and "to build." We were individually seeking support, so we formulated a peer support group. An unintentional consequence of the peer group was the creation of an Afrocentric recognized student organization that focuses on mentoring doctoral students through degree completion. The organization ensures all students involved complete their dissertation and graduate while providing academic, social, emotional, and career support. As the alumni mentor to JDA, I provide information otherwise unspoken and unwritten about career mobility and resources that were not openly shared with other higher education administrators. As a Black woman, my social responsibility is mentoring and sponsoring other Black administrators. I will continue to step up and be the change I want to see, and I encourage you to do the same.

Black women are known to be strong and resilient! We make things happen with little to nothing (Butler & Whitehead, 2021). It is known that

Black women higher education administrators face discrimination, sexism, ageism, and harmful stereotypes like the strong Black woman. Black administrators rarely access the individuals and information that can put us in a place of power or influence our career mobility. The unwritten rules and strategies are shared among those who have access to individuals with power. Every aspect of institutional culture is set up in a way that is not conducive to sharing information. Black higher education professionals are responsible for creating and maintaining opportunities that support our well-being and success in student affairs.

TIPS AND STRATEGIES

As we probe to understand Black women administrators' experience, a significant question is asked: "Did you get the memo?" As doctoral students, we learned leadership theory but were not provided strategies for operating in higher education or what to do when encountering professional obstacles (Butler & Whitehead, 2021). My life mission is to share the memo and continue using my journey to share tips and strategies to navigate higher education with others. If your doctorate is conferred, you must own your "Doctor" title/prefix and require it to be used, particularly in professional settings. Using someone's correct title/prefix is a way to respect them and create an inclusive environment by addressing them by what they want to be called. I am the change I want to see by modeling respect in a professional setting when addressing my colleagues as "Doctors" in conversations, emails, and written publications. We, as Black professionals, must show people how to treat us and create the change we want to see on college campuses when given the opportunity.

Be the Change You Want to See

The historical challenges Black women encounter in all career fields have been documented in many formats. Regardless of race, women with doctorates are met with skepticism and disrespect. The intentional act of demeaning a person's academic and professional accolades by not calling them doctors is a prime example that gender discrimination is well and alive today. To combat discrimination when you feel powerless, finding like-minded professionals for support and creating the change you want to see in the world and on college campuses is critical. As I mentioned, I cofounded JDA at USC out of needing support through the dissertation process. Fortunately, the group continues to support me postgraduation. Following the doctoral program, the founders used this network to connect one another to other scholarly and career-related opportunities (Conerly & Butler, 2020). Because finding a mentor is difficult for Black women administrators, they often seek alternative sources of support or nonacademic mentors (Patton, 2009), whether through formal or informal opportunities. Therefore, programs must be strategically developed to ensure no Black woman administrator is left behind. Furthermore, Sorcinelli and Yun (2007) summarized the importance of mentoring networks to scholars of color navigating the academic institution's complex and protean racial and gender dynamics. If you want something done, you must do it yourself by creating opportunities.

AFFIRMATION: STUDENT SUCCESS NEVER FAILS

As a student affairs professional, my work matters; whether family or friends understand my commitment to students, as a first-generation Black woman administrator who is an expert in degree completion, I am sensitive to the challenges underrepresented populations face in academia. Because higher education increases social capital and self-efficacy, student affairs practitioners are needed and valued by many students, most of whom we might never see again. I use my higher education affirmation throughout my daily interactions to stay in the student affairs profession: Student Success Never Fails! That affirmation reminds me that my hard work helping, caring, and teaching students how to persist to graduation is not in vain. As student affairs practitioners, we might not think about it often, but we transcend students' lives. When I feel discouraged or disrespected because someone called me "Miss" instead of my listed name, Dr. Butler, I remember my experiences as a student and all the higher education practitioners who helped me through my journey. Meditating over that affirmation calms me down and brings me back to my purpose in higher education, which is to pay it forward. I also created "Student Success Never Fails" posters that I have displayed in my home and work office space as a visual reminder.

CONCLUSION

I deserve to be respected and addressed by my title/prefix, "Doctor." Using counter storytelling from a CRT lens, I shared my lived experience transitioning from Miss to Doctor as a Black woman administrator in higher education. Critical race theory can be used to deconstruct the power dynamics that surround race and racism in societal structures and institutions. This theory can be helpful in understanding and transforming these power dynamics by using different methods and approaches that work towards equity and representation for minority populations (Castelli & Castelli, 2021). As members of an oppressed group, Black women must generate alternative practices that foster group empowerment (Collins, 2002).

As a first-generation Black woman administrator who is an expert in degree completion, I am sensitive to the challenges that underrepresented populations face in academia. Over the years, I have created inclusive on-campus and online environments that target minorities, veterans, and socioeconomically underprivileged students. Students, faculty, and staff consider these spaces reliable and trustworthy resources. I foster strong working relationships with campus departments, programs, and services to help me help students persist to graduation. I am an expert on self- and collective efficacy and use the theory's principles to influence work practices that increase work productivity. My educational and professional experiences indicate my ability to promote student learning, involvement, and graduation across campus. Given all my success, still in my lived experiences as a Black woman higher education practitioner, I often deal with compounded micro- and macroaggressions relating to my gender, race, and age.

To address a Black woman doctor as "Miss/Mrs.," even not knowing whether she is married, is to imply that despite her professional accomplishments, her worth is reduced to marital status. It ignores the hard work that went into earning the title of "Doctor" and denotes, whether intentional or not, that a woman with a doctorate is somehow less deserving of the title than others (Lycette, 2020). This chapter provided recommendations on creating opportunities for change, such as creating peer groups and respectfully demanding to be addressed by one's earned title/prefix "Doctor" among current and potential Black student affairs practitioners pursuing doctorate degrees. This is a call of action that the disrespect must stop!

REFERENCES

Advisory Board. (2018, November 30). *Who gets to be called "doctor?" Why the controversial question divides journalists, academics, and more* [Blog post]. Retrieved June 22, 2022, from https://www.advisory.com/daily-briefing/2018/11/30/doctor

Butler, M., & Whitehead, M. (2021). Did you get the memo? Black leadership and the climb. In H. W. Pichon & Y. Mutakabbir (Eds.), *African American leadership and mentoring through purpose, preparation, and preceptors* (pp. 101–125). IGI Global.

Castelli, M., & Castelli, M. (2021, November 4). *Introduction to critical race theory and counter-storytelling* [Blog post]. Noise Project. Retrieved June 22, 2022, from https://noiseproject.org/introduction-to-critical-race-theory-and-counter-storytelling/

Collins, P. H. (2002). *Black feminist thought: Knowledge, consciousness, and the politics of empowerment* (2nd ed.). Routledge. https://doi.org/10.4324/9780203900055

Conerly, R., & Butler, M. (2020). Who is going to mentor us? Black women administrators and our leadership journeys. In D.Cobb-Roberts & T. Esnard (Eds.), *Mentoring as critically engaged praxis: Storying the lives and contributions of Black women administrators* (pp. 47–66). Information Age Publishing.

Crenshaw, K. (1995). Mapping the margins: Intersectionality, identity politics, and violence. In K. Crenshaw, N. Gotanda, G. Peller, & K. Thomas (Eds.), *Critical race theory: The key writings that formed the movement* (pp. 357–383). New Press.

Esnard, T., & Cobb-Roberts, D. (2018). *Black women, academe, and the tenure process in the United States and the Caribbean*. Palgrave Macmillan. https://doi.org/10.1007/978-3-319-89686-1

Gregory, S. T. (2001). Black faculty women in the academy: History, status, and future. *The Journal of Negro Education, 70*(3), 124–138. https://doi.org/10.2307/3211205

Henry, W. J., & Glenn, N. M. (2009). Black women employed in the ivory tower: Connecting for success. *Advancing Women in Leadership Journal, 29*(2). https://doi.org/10.21423/awlj-v29.a271

Jean-Marie, G., & Brooks, J. S. (2011). Mentoring and supportive networks for women of color in academe. In G. Jean-Marie & B. Lloyd-Jones (Eds.), *Women of color in higher education: Changing directions and new perspectives*. Emerald Group Publishing Limited. https://doi.org/10.1108/S1479-3644(2011)0000010009

Lloyd-Jones, B. (2009). Implications of race and gender in higher education administration: An African American woman's perspective. *Advances in Developing Human Resources, 11*(5), 606–618. https://doi.org/10.1177/1523422309351820

Lovitts, B. E. (2002). *Leaving the ivory tower: The causes and consequences of departure from doctoral study*. Rowman & Littlefield Publishers.

Lycette, J. (2020, July 15). *Don't call me "Mrs." Call me "doctor."* KevinMD. Retrieved June 22, 2022, from https://www.kevinmd.com/2017/07/dont-call-mrs-call-doctor.html

Merriam-Webster. (n.d.). Persistent. In *Merriam-Webster.com dictionary*. Retrieved June 22, 2022, from https://www.merriam-webster.com/dictionary/persistence

National Center for Science and Engineering Statistics. (2021). *Survey of earned doctorates, 2020*. https://ncses.nsf.gov/pubs/nsf22300/report/u-s-doctorate-awards

Patton, L. D., & Bondi, S. (2015). Nice white men or social justice allies?: Using critical race theory to examine how white male faculty and administrators engage in ally work. *Race, Ethnicity and Education, 18*(4), 488–514. https://doi.org/10.1080/13613324.2014.1000289

Patton, L. D. (2009). My sister's keeper: A qualitative examination of mentoring experiences among African American women in graduate and professional schools. *The Journal of Higher Education, 80*(5), 510–537. https://doi.org/10.1080/00221546.2009.11779030

Sorcinelli, M. D., & Yun, J. (2007). From mentor to mentoring networks: Mentoring in the new academy. Change. *Change, 39*(6), 58–61. https://doi.org/10.3200/CHNG.39.6.58-C4

Solórzano, D. G., & Yosso, T. J. (2002). Critical race methodology: Counter-storytelling as an analytical framework for education research. *Qualitative Inquiry, 8*(1), 23–44. https://doi.org/10.1177/107780040200800103

Tomlin, A. D. (2022). I'm a Black PhD, and I still have to fight! In A. M. Allen & J. T. Stewart (Eds.), *We're not OK: Black Faculty Experiences and Higher Education Strategies* (pp. 58–74). Cambridge University Press.

Turner, C. S. V., Myers, S. L., Jr., & Creswell, J. W. (1999). Exploring underrepresentation: The case of faculty of color in the Midwest. *The Journal of Higher Education, 70*(1), 27–59. https://doi.org/10.1080/00221546.1999.11780753

SECTION II

AT THE END OF THE DAY, I GOT ME!

CHAPTER 5

HYDRATED, MOISTURIZED, AND BLACK

The Untold Story of a Black Woman Working in Career Services

Sarah L. Holliday

ABSTRACT

Working in higher education as a Black woman is a struggle. At times, you feel like you have it all together. As if you can conquer the world and everything in it. And there are other times when you feel defeated, or as if you have let down your ancestors and the legacy that you have been working on since you can remember. It's a delicate balance like a pendulum. And quite frankly, it's an ongoing act until you decide to no longer play the cat and mouse game. The game is a challenge that can uproot you, completely change you, or have you evaluating yourself daily. In hindsight, I would say that it increases your anxiety and can lead to depression, yes, I am speaking from experience.

The purpose of this chapter is to focus on the life of a Black woman working in career services and the transition of leaving higher education to pursue a career outside of education. In this chapter, we will dive into the hurts, growing pains, and successes that concluded my eight years of working in higher education. Towards the end of this chapter, I will provide tips and strategies that helped me navigate my darkest moments as I worked to achieve success and live unapologetically as my authentic self.

Still Working While Black:
The Untold Stories of Student Affairs Practitioners, pp. 39–44
Copyright © 2023 by Information Age Publishing
www.infoagepub.com

Brief Overview of Previous Positions/Careers Held

I worked in higher education for eight years and occasionally, I teach as an adjunct. I began working part-time in higher education in my mid-20's as an administrative assistant at a local community college in Maryland. Within a year, I was promoted to being a job developer. Shortly thereafter, I was hired full-time on a grant to work as a career counselor. From there, I was hired permanently as a career counselor. In total, I worked four years at the community college.

In 2014, I left the community college to pursue a career as an Assistant Director at a local university in Maryland. I was still working in career services; however, this position came with pressure and high levels of stress. It was a multifaceted position that often felt like I was the "shoulders" of the department. This position focused on areas such as: technology, programming, career development, and procurement. I held this position for four years. In 2021, I resigned from full-time employment in higher education.

One Word

There are a lot of words that come to mind when I think about my experience as a student affair professional. Words like, chaotic, detrimental, depressing, unforgettable, and faith come to mind. But, if I think a little longer, revolutionary seems like the best word to describe my experience. According to Merriam Webster, revolutionary means "constituting or bringing about a major or fundamental change" (Merriam-Webster, n.d.). And, although there were highs and lows working in higher education, the experiences, the setbacks, the stress, and the lack of support all led to a revolution. A revolution in which I took control and decided what worked best for me and walked away from anything that did not serve me best.

My revolution began during my second year working at a local university. I had a supervisor, also a Black woman, that often praised me in one breath then criticized me in another. I felt conflicted, like I needed to change who I was. It was draining, tiring, and exhausting. For two years, I had believed that I needed to work harder to prove myself and at the same time continuously show her respect because I respected the "code." And, in the Black community, the code is if one of us looks bad, we all look bad. So, I took the abuse and expressed my frustrations to family and friends. But one day, I vented to a mentor. I was sharing that I did not feel valued, that I was being bullied, constantly compared to others, told how I needed to do better, ridiculed in front of subordinates, and often overshadowed by my supervisor's ideas and opinions. And not to mention, constantly having "you aren't doing enough" thrown in my face during every 1:1 meeting. It was during this moment, that my mentor said something that sparked a revolution, "go where you are planted and build your tribe." At that moment, I felt compelled to do what was best for me. So, I resigned. Two weeks was too much time to give to a toxic and unhealthy work environment; I gave them 48 hours' notice. There are moments that I miss the students I worked with, but nothing compares to my happiness and freedom.

Challenges of My Race and Gender

There are three challenges I faced working in higher education, they are: being Black, being a woman, and being "young." However, being Black and being a woman were two of the biggest challenges. When I worked as an administrative assistant, I was often treated as the help. There were three or four full-time career counselors at the time, all of which were older White women. These women were near retirement and their work ethic, minus one of them, was often a reflection. As an administrative assistant, I was responsible for maintaining the office, hiring student employees, training student employees, organizing meetings, placing food orders, and so on.

I recall sitting in a meeting roughly a month after starting my position. My supervisor, a Black male, had not arrived and he asked me to start the meeting. I handed out the agendas and began introducing myself to break the ice. Midway into my introduction, one of the ladies said, "You're the first Black woman I have seen in our office. It's obvious you are the administrative assistant and not one of us." I paused. What was I supposed to say? This had been my first time hearing these words, especially in a meeting. I looked at her, my eyes were drilled into her soul, I could see the resentment written all over her face. I replied, "Out of curiosity, what exactly do you mean? If it's a matter of education, I have that. If it's a matter of position, I have no interest in filling your shoes. Please, let's continue."

Now, you may think, why didn't I completely tell her about herself or report her? Well, the reality is that I wasn't prepared for that moment, nor did I know I had the right to report her. More than anything, I was concerned about keeping my job. I had a semester left of grad school and this job was paying the bills. So, I did what I believed was right at the time. And, when I had the chance, I spoke with my supervisor privately about this situation. From there, he connected me to other Black women in higher education who in turn served as mentors.

Opportunities That My Race and Gender

Being a Black woman is magical. It's a great feeling. Our melanin is always poppin', our hips and curves adore any garment of clothing, and our demeanor is poised, elegant, and nurturing. Black women are the real MVP's, we are the G.O.A.T. Working in higher education afforded me the ability to work with men and women that were transparent, helpful, encouraging, and supportive. When I first began working in higher education, I was naive, nervous, and hopeful. I had numerous ideas of how to improve education and help our students. I also had thoughts of helping minorities and increasing their graduation and retention rates. As I expressed these ideas, I started making connections with deans, vice presidents, faculty, and other student affairs practitioners. I started networking and building a tribe of people that looked like me, talked like me, but could also help me. I confided in them, listened to their words of advice, and sought their ongoing support.

My race and gender afforded the opportunity to obtain grants and scholarships to attend conferences where I learned from practitioners that incorporated change. My race and gender became an example to students regarding hard work and dedication. It afforded the opportunity to teach literacy and writing skills to minority students, career courses to uncertain students, freshman seminar to new students, and life skills to students experiencing hopelessness.

Tips/Strategies

Working in higher education can be a great experience. As with any employer or industry, there are highs, lows, difficult people, unfair situations, and so on. Below are a few tips or strategies that I would like to suggest for current or potential student affairs practitioners.

1. **Meditate/Pray**—Channel your inner thoughts and focus; center yourself. Meditation provides the opportunity to block out the noise and focus inward. What are you saying to yourself? Are you being kind to yourself? What is bothering you? What is contributing to your anxiety or frustrations? As you meditate, pray or some people chant. Whatever you need to do to clear your mind and remember the amazing person you are, do it. Meditation/prayer should be a daily self-care ritual. It's necessary!

2. **Build Your Tribe**—Surround yourself with people that will help you, encourage you, mentor you, and praise you. Your tribe is your support system and should be a group of people you trust and confide in. Your tribe should be diverse in educational level, career, race, gender, and so on. You need a diverse outlook on life and in your career.

3. **It's Chess, Not Checkers**—As with anything in life, you must be prepared. While everyone is playing the cat and mouse game or telephone, you play chess. You learn your opponents and play to their strengths and weaknesses. Your mission or vision is your focus, so you remove yourself from anything or anyone that does not align with it.

4. **Protect Your Peace**—Sometimes, life is a battlefield. The key is surrounding yourself with peace and joy. Doing this requires that you do what is best for you and forsake what everyone wants you to do. If you feel uncertain, restless, and so on, in certain situations or around certain people, leave it alone. Your peace is your inner voice or intuition speaking to you, listen and be guided by it.

5. **Network**—Closed mouths don't get fed. If you're like me, networking can be difficult, but it is also necessary. Your network is your net worth. Talk to people, learn about them, stay connected to them. Job opportunities are often shared in circles or within networks. So, network and join professional associations, they are very helpful! My network helped me change careers!

6. **Have a career goal**—There's nothing wrong with a career goal. Goals motivate us and reduce complacency. Think about where you want to be in one year, three years, five, years, and so on, and develop a game plan to achieve those goals. You got this!

7. **Practice Self-care and Have Fun!**—All work and no play isn't a balanced life. Take time for you and rejuvenate. Take a day trip, do a spa day, go walking, jogging, and so on. Find an outlet so that you can unplug and rest. Make sure it's relaxing but also fun. You work hard, make sure you play hard.

Affirmation

Affirmations are a blessing! They are powerful, uplifting, positive things that help you through your darkest moments and most difficult times. Here are a few affirmations that have helped me.

1. **I deserve happiness, joy, abundance, and overflow.** When I started therapy, this was the first self-affirmation I wrote in purple lipstick. I wrote it on my bathroom mirror. It was an affirmation I said every morning and every night. It was a reminder of what I deserve and was motivation for me to continue moving forward.

2. **Tears are a sign of strength, not weakness.** When I started having issues at the university, I cried often. Mostly at home or in my car. I set this as a reminder on my phone to let me know that I wasn't weak but strong. It was something that resonated with me after my last therapy session. I had finished two years of therapy and just started with a life coach. This was one of the first things she said to me, and it has remained with me. When we cry, our body lets go of whatever is bothering us and in turn, we gain clarity.

Conclusion

I am grateful for the experiences I learned while working as a student affairs practitioner. Although there were dark moments, there were also times that I laughed uncontrollably, cried happy tears silently, and rejoiced publicly. One of my happiest moments was commencement. Seeing all the students smile walking across the stage and their parents cheering for them was heartwarming. Another happy moment was cheering for the student that got their dream job or internship and hugging them as they cried tears of joy. Every moment as a Black student affairs practitioner was rewarding both the good and the bad. However, at some point, as I used to tell my students, we must take a "leap of faith." And although I sincerely miss the students I worked with and a few colleagues I connected with, I had to do what was best for me. So, after several therapy conversations, sleepless nights, prayer, fasting, and journaling, I left higher education. I revised my resume, learned new skills, and transitioned to a career in technology. And, I have no regrets. Every disappointment led to a beautiful and well-deserved lucrative career in a field that I enjoy and with a company that values its employees.

REFERENCE

Merriam-Webster. (n.d.). Revolution. In *Merriam-Webster*. Retrieved May 24, 2022, from https://www.merriam-webster.com/dictionary/revolutionary

CHAPTER 6

Y'ALL ARE NOT ABOUT TO WORRY ME

Grace Is Extended to Everyone Except Black Women

Eboni Chism, Jamie J. Doss, and Erica McBride

ABSTRACT

Why didn't they tell us this part? Too many Black women in student affairs are unrecognized, undercompensated, and undervalued for their invisible labor. As Black women at Predominantly White Institutions, we often become mentors, coaches, and support systems for not just Black students, but all students of color. Black women come into academic spaces and already have negative connotations associated with them. Being a Black woman, actively navigating our Black identity is hard, when you have students who do not see their privileges. This chapter explores the experiences of three Black women in their early careers, as student affairs professionals. We illustrate how we find our voice, advocate for our Blackness, and carry the weight of invisible labor, within predominantly White spaces.

INTRODUCTION AND OVERVIEW

Black women often acknowledge and understand their intelligence and that they have the skills needed to be successful in their given area. We know this because we have the degree, skills, and work experience to validate

Still Working While Black:
The Untold Stories of Student Affairs Practitioners, pp. 45–58
Copyright © 2023 by Information Age Publishing
www.infoagepub.com

this evidence. Black women navigating oppressive spaces are left to juggle with how they cope with their experiences of racial and gender oppression. Being a Black woman and serving as a student affairs professional at a predominantly White institution (PWI) is no easy feat. Our intersecting identity (Crenshaw, 1991) requires a certain temperament and level of confidence to navigate a system of higher education that oppresses Black women and other individuals of color. Due to these experiences, Black women in student affairs put into question their academic capabilities, making them feel the need to hide who they are in the presence of our White peers and faculty. This has caused them to create a mask to hide our vulnerabilities as a way to survive the emotional and mental stressors we experience due to racial and gendered microaggressions.

All three authors have worked in student affairs in different capacities and are enrolled in a PhD in higher education program at a Midwest private higher education institution. Eboni has served as an academic success advisor and coach at two predominantly White higher education institutions for the past four years, specifically serving the low socioeconomic and nontraditional adult population. In addition, she currently serves as adjunct for a first-year student success course. I am an African American woman and I have worked in higher education for a little over four years. I began my journey into student affairs while working as the front desk receptionist at my high school. I guess you can say the interest in this field "fell into my lap" because I truly enjoyed the relationships I cultivated when students came into the office. The conversations we had and stories we shared had absolutely nothing to do with my job, but I enjoyed them so much and I would like to think that the students enjoyed them as well. They continued to come back. I also knew that I wanted to go back to school for master's, so without any idea of what I was applying for and getting myself into, I found myself sitting in my first class for the College Student Personnel Administration master's program. A year into my graduate program, I started my career in student affairs as an academic advisor at a community college, where I worked with primarily low income, nontraditional, first generational, and trade program students. As I continue my career in the area of advising and student success, I currently work for a large four-year private nonprofit Jesuit institution as an academic coach, serving nontraditional students in online degree programs while also pursuing my doctoral degree in the School of Education in the Higher Education Administration program, where I met Jamie and Erica.

Jamie is a Licensed Clinical Professional Counselor that served as a Career Counselor for four years at a predominantly White public institution providing a myriad of career and academic services to students and alumni. I currently serve in a human resources capacity at a predominantly White private institution. Prior to entering student affairs, I worked in the mental health and nonprofit sector providing individual counseling, case management, career and academic coaching, and crisis counseling. The population I served was predominantly students with diagnosed disabilities and co-occurring mental health disorders. I greatly enjoyed assisting these individuals with navigating their academic programs and achieving their career goals, but I desired to do this work on a larger scale and expand the population I served. My passion for lifelong learning also contributed to my desire to shift my efforts towards serving in a student services capacity in higher education. During my third year of serving in student affairs, I began pursuing my doctoral degree in Higher Education Administration where I had the privilege of meeting Eboni and Erica. Although I am no longer serving in student affairs, my passion for higher education has not waivered and it remains strong. I am proud to be a member of this community as a human resources professional, doctoral student and lifelong learner.

Erica is a social worker who serves a Program Coordinator within the Division of Innovation and Community Engagement for the MLK Scholars Program and Safe Zone Competency within a PWI. During this role I structure programs and initiative for LGBTQ+ students and students who are dedicated to social justice and community service. Prior to this role I was the first coordinator within a biology department within a predominantly White university. I assisted first generation students and students of color with navigating STEM disciplines. Erica has been in higher education for two years and prior to working within education, I served as a case manager for people with intellectual and developmental disabilities. With the shift from being a case manager to working with higher education, I began my passion for diversity, equity, and inclusion. During my first year of being within higher education, I started my PhD program within higher education administration.

Our goal in collaborating on this chapter is to authentically illuminate the opportunities and challenges our race and gender have brought to our professional experiences as Black women student affairs practitioners at predominantly White higher education institutions. We hope that by offering insight into who we are and where we are in our professional careers, much like the field of student affairs, that our experiences as early career professionals and Black women bring a unique yet just as important narrative. Additionally, we aim to encourage Black women student affairs professionals, just as ourselves, to embrace and adapt their true authentic selves.

PERSONAL NARRATIVES

In this chapter of *Still Working While Black: The Untold Stories of Student Affairs Practitioners*, we each provide personal narratives of our experiences as Black women student affairs practitioners. We each offer one word that describes our experiences as student affairs practitioners, which is then followed by our individual reflections on the importance of the word. Throughout our personal narratives, we illuminate some of the opportunities and challenges our race and gender have brought to our professional experiences as student affairs practitioners. We also suggest strategies to help current and future Black student affairs professionals navigate the dynamics of this predominantly White field of higher education.

Eboni

One Word to Describe My Experience in Student Affairs

If I could use one word to describe the experience of my journey as a student affairs professional that word would be unapologetic. Growing up in a predominantly White community, attending a predominantly White school district, growing up with predominantly White friends, and maybe even to my own naive fault, I never knew how much less was I aware of the ability to be unapologetically Black. The ability to adapt in these spaces, spaces where I adapted so well, led to me being compared to other people who were "Blacker" than me. It also led me to believe that my success within other career areas was not because of my true self, but rather as to who I could perceive myself as. Strange right? Who would think a shift in higher education would be where I would discover my authentic self? Coincidentally my first position as an academic advisor at a mid-Western predominantly White community college, I was blessed, and highly favored, with the opportunity to work with an array of Black women. It was the first time I had ever worked in the same space with so many women that looked like me, who shared many of my same experiences with whom I could relate to as a Black woman, and a Black mother raising a teenage Black son. This was a space and an experience I was missing but never knew I needed. The stories we shared were Black, the advice we gave was Black. Blackity, Black.... Black, Black. There wasn't a specific conversation or statement made that changed how I saw myself. It was a feeling. A natural internal development of who I was as a Black woman. I knew a little bit more about who I was, and I was a little more confident in who I could be. Growing up, I knew I wanted to be something different, but I wasn't sure

in what respect that difference would be. I didn't see very many successful Black women and the women in my family were continuously working
dead jobs and unhappy. Working with other Black women who shared the
experiences, who motivated and mentored me, was a liberating feeling. I
not only saw my previous self in my students, but I also saw my future self in
the Black women I worked with. Student success and support can get busy,
you will be overworked, and short staffed. This experience brought me to
a place where I just wanted to give up, but the encouragement and support
from my Black female colleagues allowed me to press forward through the
stress to get me where I am in my career and education today.

Challenges

Collins's (2000) defines self-definition as a process or "journey to a free
mind" (p. 112) away from internalized oppression, or seeing ourselves
how others see us, in a sense of race, class, gender, and sexuality. From the
way we behave, dress, look, and speak, for generations Black women have
been taught that to be just as successful as our white counterparts, we must
hide our cultural nuances, and adapt the behaviors of the more dominant
White culture, because it is what society deemed as the norm. However,
when we adapt this unapologetic concept, we are leaving ourselves open
and vulnerable.

As freeing as my unapologetic self sounds, challenges occurred when I
had to hold some of that in because I wasn't quite sure of myself. Many challenges arose when I wasn't sure if I was being too unapologetic and being
too free or secure in myself as a Black woman. Knowing and understanding when to turn it off, when to hold it in, was I too Black for the student
that isn't Black or a student of color is what I pondered. I searched for
the self-doubt I previously tucked away, to find the mask I hid behind and
wore so well. It wasn't until my social justice in higher education course in
my doctoral program that I really learned and understood what racial and
gendered microaggressions were. The crazy part is that the more research I
read, the more aware I became of my interactions with my White peers. The
biggest challenges I've faced and continue to fear are unexpected microaggressions. It is easy to find yourself in a space that requires you to always
be prepared. That is, prepared for the microaggressive comments that you
always hear. The comments I did not expect at that moment were, and still
are challenging to navigate because I am not sure how to respond. The
microaggressive comments were not always towards me but also towards
certain aspects of the Black culture. From the "I don't have White privilege
because I grew up in a trailer park" to the "why was Mary J in the halftime

show? She can't dance anymore and she's too old to be wearing those small clothes" comments, it can be overwhelming and exhausting.

Another challenge is the facial expressions and change in attitudes parents would make because my voice and face didn't match with what they were expecting to see. I remember talking with a parent on the phone about helping to get their student registered for classes. The conversation was great, and to go above and beyond, I told the parents to specifically ask for me when they came in so that I could finish helping them. To my not so expectant surprise, I was met with an "Wait your Eboni?" Yes, I am the person you spoke with on the phone. To be honest, I enjoyed those moments. It was like I was giving an impromptu learning lesson. Not all Black people sound alike. In fact, we can camouflage our voices within different spaces. Was my name not ethnic enough? I mean, my name speaks for itself. Once we were in my office the vibe changed. It seemed like she questioned every comment I made. It was exhausting and all I could think about were the endless nights I spent writing papers, using vacation and sick time to complete final projects, commenting to two or three of my peers in a discussion post, all to sit here and have a parent question every word, as if what I was saying wasn't valid. Why didn't they teach us this in grad school? Yes, student affairs is a broad field, but professionals of color have different experiences than each other and their non-colleagues of color. Then I remembered, none of my professors looked like me, so how would they have even known how vital this information could have been. These moments serve as a reminder of the importance of my Black presence in student affairs, my motivation to stay in the field of student affairs, and my ambition behind teaching and mentoring other Black student affairs professionals.

Opportunities

There are many things that make up the identity of a Black woman, their roles as mothers, daughters, granddaughters, wives, and professionals. As Black student affairs professional, we engage with so many different students and hold so many different roles. Especially for many of our students who look like us and share our experiences. If we don't have the ability to be comfortable and confident in ourselves, how can we essentially help our students who look like us? My ability to navigate my workspace as an unapologetic Black woman, also gives me the courage to share my stories of success with the student who crossed my path that not only looked like me but reminded me of myself throughout my educational journey. A single mother, trying to make school and responsibilities work. I was no longer ashamed of my downfalls; I was no longer embarrassed by the financial mistakes I made. The energy of being my unapologetic Black-self also allowed my students to be vulnerable with me and for them to embrace the "real" conversations we had. The "So what we are not gon do," "Let's get it in order" hard conversations is what led my students to feel more motivated and acknowledge the changes that needed to be made for their success.

Affirmation

> "When you walk your steps will not be hindered, and when you run, you will not stumble"
>
> —Proverbs 4:12

Through the years I learned to not only apply my spiritual growth to my personal life, but my professional life as well. Student affairs was not a career I planned for. Admittedly, when I made the shift, I had no idea what I was getting myself into. All I knew was that I had a passion for helping others navigate their success and help them see the potential I saw in them. This scripture, among others, sits on the bottom of my monitor along with other random sticky note reminders of who to reach out to and what to do. It is a daily reminder that although there are challenges, there are always opportunities to turn them into tools for my success. My students keep me going. Their stories keep me going.

Jamie

One Word to Describe My Experience in Student Affairs

As I reflect on my experience as a Black woman student affairs practitioner, a myriad of words come to mind but one that has the most meaning to my experience is: undervalued. I connect my experience in student affairs to this term because it represents the lack of genuine appreciation and recognition, I experienced during my tenure in student affairs. To relate this experience to theory, I endured marginality and a lack of mattering. Schlossberg (1989) outlined in her theory the importance of all students feeling valued, accepted, and a sense of mattering to help combat the overt marginalization and otherness they experience at PWIs. I believe this theory is also applicable to minoritized professionals working in higher education. Although marginality and a lack of mattering are often permanent conditions for minoritized individuals, the overt marginalization, and toxic environments they experience in predominantly White spaces exacerbates these conditions and has the potential to negatively impact their development and success. Although I endured this type of environment while serving in student affairs, I knew my value and the unique skill set I leveraged to help the institution achieve its mission. It was the mission, the students, my level of confidence, and my passion for higher education that helped sustain my commitment to the field. In addition, my desire to serve as a conduit for change that challenges systems of power, privilege and oppression in higher education served as a motivator to persist in higher education despite challenges and uncomfortable situations.

Challenges

Serving in student affairs as an early career Black woman came with many challenges. One of those challenges was invisible labor. As a Black woman student affairs practitioner at a PWI, and the only person of color in the Career Services department, I also served as a mentor, coach, and support system for Black students, other students of color, and White students. I also became the department expert and go-to for all things diversity, equity, and inclusion (DEI) based on my race and gender. I took on these roles because I wanted to foster the growth and development of all students and advance the institution towards becoming a model of inclusive excellence. However, I rarely experienced any recognition, appreciation, or compensation from the institution for the extra service I provided despite my extensive workload. This made me feel undervalued and unsupported in my efforts to help the institution accomplish its mission. Over time, I became numb to the lack of recognition and appreciation from the university. I speculate that administrators believed the appreciation I received from students and colleagues was sufficient, but this was further from the truth. Being undervalued in student affairs is one of the reasons I elected to leave the division despite a continued passion for the mission of student affairs and the students I served.

Despite individual efforts to increase the number of Black faculty and staff in higher education, this population remains disproportionately underrepresented in the higher education workforce (Reames, 2021). According to the College and University Professional Association for Human Resources (CUPA-HR, 2020), Black and African American employees make up less than 10% of higher education professionals (CUPA-HR, 2020). This was the case at the institution I served at while working in student affairs. It was lonely being the only Black professional in my department and one of approximately five Black administrative professional staff in student affairs. I found it challenging to navigate certain situations in my department and in the division out of fear of retaliation and losing opportunities that I enjoyed and that contributed to my professional development. I had to find a way to choreograph my actions and steps in a way that illuminated my value and labor to those that chose to be oblivious to it. That required the transparency, authenticity, and a high-level of confidence that I developed and fostered while serving in student affairs.

Opportunities

Despite the challenges previously outlined, there were many opportunities that my race and gender afforded me during my career in student affairs. The roles I took on that ultimately reflected invisible labor were opportunities I was given because of my positionality as a Black professional woman. I was able to serve as a mentor to minoritized students, provide DEI best practices and trainings within my department and division, and serve on university committees focused on advancing various DEI initiatives. These opportunities allowed me to contribute to systemic change and dismantle racism through education, advocacy, and mobilization. My positionality also afforded me the opportunity to serve as a champion for students of color and those from disadvantaged backgrounds. These were meaningful experiences to empower, support, and advocate on behalf of a vulnerable population of students, faculty, and staff that otherwise would remain marginalized. It was and continues to be an honor to use my voice and experiences in higher education to center the voices of the minoritized and the inequities they experience. This opportunity is one that remains salient throughout my professional journey in higher education.

Affirmation

During my career in student affairs and in my personal life, an affirmation that centers me is a quote by Harry and Rosemary Wong (2018) in their book *The First Days of School: How to Be an Effective Teacher*, "Whoever is doing all the work is doing all the learning." This quote is extremely meaningful to me as it connects to my passion for lifelong learning and reminds me that all my hard work contributes to my learning and development. Moreover, it adds depth to my knowledge that will help me impact the lives of others and higher education as a whole. Some individuals store affirmations on notepads, on their phone screensaver, or calendar, but this particular affirmation is stored in my memory. I have shared this quote with others in different venues, as it serves as a great motivator to remain engaged in the work, we are passionate about while learning in the process.

Erica

One Word to Describe My Experience in Student Affairs

Being a Black woman in academia in a predominantly White space has its challenges and so many words come into play that it becomes indescribable in a sense. When thinking of one word that can define my experience within higher education, I would have to say unworthy. Though this word has a negative connotation, that's exactly how I feel. If you're too outspoken you are labeled as loud, aggressive, or combative. If you are too soft spoken, then you are deemed too incompetent to lead. There is no straightforward way to please people within higher education. If being Black in America wasn't hard enough, then imagine being Black in predominantly White spaces majority of each and every day. Jim Crow laws, Ruby Bridges, affirmative action, *Brown vs. the Board of Education*, and so forth, imagine all of this and still in this day and age, not feeling welcomed or recognized within a place; or rather a system that was never designed for you. Black administrators, faculty, and staff are the Black faces students feel supported by; we are the mothers away from home, we are the administrators who hold the pieces of the institution together. Though I know I am worthy of being within predominantly White spaces and fully capable of roles I have within higher education, I feel as if I am seen as unworthy by students and other leaders. This comes from the way in which privilege is displayed in every space I walk into.

Challenges

Black women come into academic spaces and already have negative connotations associated with them. We are already labeled as loud, aggressive, mean, and deemed unable to complete our roles. Though we typically do more duties than required, we are not compensated the same as White men and women, or Black men. We don't receive the same grace that students nor any other university members receive. When we feel overwhelmed and stressed, we are taught to push through which goes back to historical context. We are taught to be strong and resilient, advocate for everyone and to endure anything life throws at us and to not fuss about it. When we do speak up, we are labeled as combative and receive backlash or possibly other consequences, just for the way society views and labels Black women. This makes me feel like no matter what I do nothing is ever good enough. Black women always have to go above and beyond; yet we still are never seen as good enough. Students are able to disrespect or treat me any way they deem fit in certain situations. When I deem it is necessary to speak up, I am often labeled as aggressive, hostile and insensitive. As a Black woman I feel as if I never get passes and I am never are able to stay "I am struggling," without fearing that I will possibly lose my job for doing so. I don't get "mental health breaks" nor can I come to White spaces and "have a bad day." Though others can and are extended grace, I am not allowed to bring personal issues to work, nor can I make excuses.

Though I am a Black woman attending a PWI, some Black students don't speak to me when I speak first. These are things I endured during my undergraduate experience as well. I am my true authentic self in all realms and do not feel the need to code switch and/or change to fit into White spaces. Some Black people frown upon this and may feel like I am someone they don't want to associate with. This makes me feel like I don't belong and less than. I have simply said "hi" to a few Black PhD students and they don't respond but speak to our White colleagues. Maybe they feel like I'm the "stereotypical Black girl," or maybe they feel as if I don't belong in the program for whatever reason. I have been called ghetto by other Black peers within higher education but regardless of how I appear or come off I am in the same spot as others for a reason. There is often a division within the Black community based on ways in which one acts and where they are in life overall. There's no winning when you try to better yourself. Either you're a sellout, conforming to White societal norms, too woke or too Black. It's draining.

Opportunities

Though I have expressed several challenges within higher education there are also many opportunities for growth. Though there are other ways to fund higher education, if I did not work within higher education, I doubt I would be in a doctoral program. Opportunities such as tuition remission, professional development, mentorship and supporting students are always advantages I ponder upon. I have had the opportunity to work within an all-White space as well as a diverse space within higher education. Though both roles included implementing diversity, equity, and inclusion initiatives; I received an opportunity to see how higher education operates systematically and behind the scenes. Seeing the way predominantly White divisions are compensated more, given more resources and the way in which they advocate for their students gave me the opportunity to learn more as I grow into a leader and professional within higher education. Being a Black cisgender woman, I understand my limitations, but I also understand my privileges.

Though I still am undervalued, not always heard, sometimes seen as incompetent or as a way in which higher education reaches their diversity quota, I'm also inspirational. To come from an underserved community, attending underserved public schools for K–12, then attending an honors college, obtaining a master's and now in a PhD program is rare. People like me who grew up in the environment I did, didn't have support, tools, or resources, and were often ruled out and made into a statistic. Me being present, as my full and true authentic self resonates better with first- generation, low income, and students of color. I can't win every battle I face but I can show students that you are worthy of being in this fight with me.

Affirmation

Martin Luther King, Jr. once said, "Almost always, the creative, dedicated minority has made the world better." I love this quote as I feel like change doesn't start with teams, groups or "higher ups." It starts with one person who takes a stand and says I want better, and I deserve better. That one person who thinks differently, looks different, speaks different, behaves differently in an act of resistance from what society deems "fit, worthy or right" creates the change we need in this world. Whether that change be big or small it is always remarkable and contiguous. If students and institutions don't see us making the change or amplifying our voices, then no progress will be made. We are the change and simply being present is enough to shift the culture towards inclusivity.

TIPS AND STRATEGIES

To fully adapt to creating a true sense of self, Black women need to be the company of a collective community where they have free voice, autonomy, and the ability to move towards a liberated mind. The implementation of support groups and/or faculty mentorship can foster this growth and development. Therefore, we encourage you to find your people and don't be afraid to make connections. There are not many of us, but we are here, there, and everywhere. Don't be afraid to ask about or seek out Black faculty and staff organizations on your campus. There is power in your collective voice. This is true, especially if you are the only one who looks like you and there is no one to share your experiences with. A podcast we would like to mention is Blk Womyn Voices podcast. This podcast specifically addresses the challenges and opportunities of Black women in student affairs and in higher education.

Additionally, speak up early so that you do not fall into the trap of invisible labor. Furthermore, be in tune with your limits and when your plate is full. Do not allow yourself to be pressured or made to feel guilty for saying no to an opportunity that you cannot take on at the moment. We are reminded by our mentors that "no" is an answer and we should use it when necessary. We extend this same advice to current and future Black student affairs practitioners trying to find the balance in their service to others. Even if grace is not extended to you at your higher education institution, remember to extend it to yourself because you deserve it!

Another recommendation is to remain your authentic self. The environment you are in or entering has the potential to cause assimilation which ultimately does not benefit the institution or the students it serves. When we show up as our authentic selves in spaces where we are expected to assimilate, it creates a sense of uncomfortableness for certain individuals. But that is when true learning and change can occur. Be yourself, be transparent, and follow through on the mission you set out to accomplish in this field. Navigating student affairs and the academy as Black woman is a lot of trial and error. What works today, may not work tomorrow, but you should remain steadfast, resilient, and intentional in your approach.

CONCLUSION AND FINAL THOUGHTS

Being a Black woman student affairs professional in predominantly White spaces comes with opportunities and challenges. However, the challenges can be overcome with intentionality, commitment, authentic confidence, and a plan to navigate obstacles as they arise. Failure is likely to occur along the journey, but failure often gets us closer to achieving our goals by strengthening best practices such as perseverance and resilience. As Black women we also have to remember that we matter and our influence matters. As important as it is to find others who we connect with, we also must acknowledge that not all experiences are the same and not everyone is ready to comfortably embrace their authenticity. You may even be met with opposition from those who look just like you. As we dismantle systematic barriers and oppression, we continue to amplify our voices to display our leadership and create a sense of belonging. Our ancestors built these institutions and fought for us to be in the places we are today. We see our privilege in the ability to fight an ongoing battle to show that though these spaces weren't designed for us, we are shifting the cultural norms and taking back our power.

REFERENCES

College and University Professional Association for Human Resources (CUPA-HR). (2020). *The Black and White higher education workforce*. CUPA-HR. Retrieved March 31, 2022, from https://www.cupahr.org/surveys/research-briefs/2020-the-black-and-white-higher-education-workforce/

Collins, P. H. (2000). *Black feminist thought: knowledge, consciousness, and the politics of empowerment*. Routledge.

Crenshaw, K. (1991). Mapping the margins: Intersectionality, identity politics, and violence against women of color. *Stanford Law Review, 43*(6), 1241–1299.

Reames, T. G. (2021). A call for authentic Black engagement in the academy and beyond. *Nature Human Behaviour, 5*, 2. https://doi.org/10.1038/s41562-020-00984-8

Schlossberg, N. K. (1989). Marginality and mattering: Key issues in building community. *New Directions for Higher Education, 48*, 5– 15.

Wong, H. K., & Wong, R. T. (2018). *The first days of school: How to be an effective teacher*. Harry K. Wong Publications.

CHAPTER 7

FROM PET TO THREAT

When Black Excellence Places You in Peril in the Workplace

Dana G. Stilley

ABSTRACT

This chapter will highlight the lived experiences of the author during her tenure while employed in various student affairs positions at a midsized community college. As an African American woman who is uniquely situated in two historically disadvantaged social constructs, namely race and gender, the author reflects on her exclusive experiences which were impacted by the intersection of her race and gender, and how her experiences may have influenced her ascension, effectiveness, leadership, and retention in student affairs leadership roles.

About Me

My entry into higher education occurred after an extensive, successful career on Wall Street. I began my higher education career as an adjunct instructor at a community college, when I responded to a call from the college president at that time, who was working diligently to increase the diversity of the faculty. After a short time serving as an adjunct instructor, I accepted a per diem job in student affairs to address organizational inadequacies in the admissions office of the college. Over the next several years,

Still Working While Black:
The Untold Stories of Student Affairs Practitioners, pp. 59–68
Copyright © 2023 by Information Age Publishing
www.infoagepub.com

I was offered and accepted jobs with greater responsibilities and leadership opportunities at the same institution. I held the following positions: Recruitment Specialist, Interim Dean of Enrollment Management, Dean of Enrollment Management, Associate Vice President of Student Services and Vice President of Enrollment Management and Student Services.

Recently I completed my doctoral program and earned a PhD in community college leadership. Currently I serve as an adjunct instructor at a four-year institution. Additionally, I am the founder and CEO of The Stilley Agency, an educational consulting company specializing in academic editing and dissertation coaching. I continue to explore research opportunities that focus on telling the stories and experiences of African American women in leadership.

Opportunities Abound

My entrance into a career in higher education was completely unplanned and totally unexpected. I can still recall how hesitant I was when I accepted my first job as an adjunct instructor for a higher education institution. I had no formal training or instruction, nor had I ever created a syllabus or a course outline. While I had extensive tutoring experience, at no time had I ever formally instructed or managed a classroom. To add to my concerns, my orientation to the job was lackluster. I could sense that the department chair was going through the motions but had no real interest in ensuring that I felt welcomed into the fold and was prepared to meet my students in just a few days. After approximately 30 minutes with the chair, I left with a copy of the textbook, and little else. Truth be told, I was hired because there was a need, and the President wanted that need filled by a person of color.

Nevertheless, I overcame my trepidation about teaching for two distinct reasons. First, I was confident that I was a content expert, having excelled in the discipline since I was a young child. I knew the course content like the back of my hand, and that confidence propelled me to overcome any anxiety I felt due to my lack of teaching experience. I channeled the expertise I garnered from previous presentations and dove right in. Second, I understood the importance of representation and the need for faculty diversity. The success of students is directly correlated with their ability to see and interact with faculty that look like them.

The positive effects of building diversity into faculty and higher education staff, as well as educational programming, has been affirmed in extant research. Increased diversity points to a positive influence in teaching, learning, and the persistence and retention of the student body (Bowman, 2011; Levine, 1991; Tienta, 2013). In addition to enhancing the ability to relate to a diverse student body, diversity in administrative leadership creates new cultural perspectives and enables trustworthy policy formation and responsible decision making (Nevarez & Santamaria, 2010; Wrighten, 2018). The lack of diversity in the ranks of faculty and administrators is one of the most important contemporary issues facing higher education.

The opportunity to teach allowed me to not only increase my professional skills, but also to enrich the college's faculty. It was my desire to become a great instructor, and be a source of encouragement to all students, especially to students of color. It did not take me long to discover that I was functioning in a silo. I was the only African American woman instructor, full-time or part-time, in the entire department. I was never evaluated or given any feedback regarding my performance. I had no mentor, and never heard of any professional development opportunities. I went to campus to teach my courses and had very little interaction with anyone other than my students.

A short time after I began teaching an opportunity presented itself to provide administrative support to the college after several operational deficiencies were identified in the admissions department. As the college sought to make managerial changes, I was asked to review operations and practices, as a per diem employee. My initial tasks were to observe the daily functions of staff, review the mechanics and implementation of the customer relationship management system and provide feedback to my supervisor, the Dean. As a per diem, lower-level employee in student affairs, I presented no threat. I was given a little autonomy to investigate practices and then report my findings to my supervisor. Using skills adapted and honed during my previous career, I was able to quickly identify much needed modifications that would enhance the enrollment business practices.

During this time, the Dean and I developed a successful working relationship built upon mutual respect and trust. While this did not happen overnight, her support and trust in my abilities were extremely instrumental in my success at that institution. She taught me a great deal about student services, and the inner workings of higher education. But, when she offered me a position as a recruitment specialist, I must admit that I was disappointed. I felt like I was extremely overqualified for that job. As I considered my options, I thought about the "good" work that I could accomplish by assisting students with their entry into higher education. I already had a good relationship with the Dean, and the idea of making a difference in students' lives weighed heavily on me. I accepted the job and my career in student affairs began to move along a very fast track.

The opportunities seemed to abound. Within seven years I had ascended through the ranks of Dean and Associate Vice President to become the Vice President of Student Services. As the Vice President of Student Services, I was ultimately responsible for Admissions, Financial Aid, the Registrar, Athletics, Accessibility Services, Veterans Affairs, Counseling, and everything else related to student support and student leadership. I believed that I was equipped and ready to effectively lead and positively impact the lives of the students. I had earned a seat at the table, and my voice would be heard. I was the college's choice. I was celebrated and in good standing with the faculty and other administrators. I certainly felt like a favorite. I had no inkling of the challenges that I was about to face.

Not One, Not Two, But Many

The challenges of African American women in leadership in higher education have been well documented. The most notable challenges include managing experiences related to invisibility, isolation, marginalization, the glass ceiling, organizational structure, stereotyping, discrimination, meritocracy, and sexism and racism (Baxter-Nuamah, 2015; Braxton, 2018; Hylton, 2012; Jones, 2013; Knowles & Lowery, 2012; Schultz, 2015; Stilley, 2021; Tomlin, 2022; Waring, 2003). My experiences did not differ from many of those noted above.

When I was appointed, I took the place of the woman who had served as my supervisor since I began my work in student services. She was a strong, White woman who also had risen through the ranks from the Dean position. She was opinionated, serious, and tough, yet extremely student centered. She was well respected for her work ethic and the ability to get things done. Over the years we had become true friends. When she retired and I became the Vice President, the college did not backfill the Associate Vice President position that I vacated. It simply disappeared. With no Deans in place, I functioned without adequate secondary leadership to the sub-departments of Enrollment Management and Student Affairs for too long. In the beginning I was too blinded by the excitement of the new position to realize the impossibility of successfully managing a division with little to no support.

Unlike my predecessor, who had me as her AVP, I was now maintaining the workload that was previously held by her and I. I worked all the time—doing the wrong things. There was always a fire to put out, a staffing issue, or a meeting to attend. I had very little time to devote to leadership; thinking, redeveloping, and planning. There was no time or energy left to develop, communicate, and implement a vision for the division. My leadership expertise was stifled, and I struggled to not be reduced to just a problem solver. Even the addition of one Dean position still did not provide sufficient support.

This situation like countless others that I experienced resulted from the intersection of my race and gender. In this instance the college seemed to have consciously, or subconsciously, endorsed the Strong Black woman stereotype, trusting that I had exceptional strength and could successfully assume multiple roles. What is equally upsetting is the realization that I too accepted the strong Black woman race-gender schema and bore some responsibility for allowing that situation to last as long as it did. I was overpowered by the idea that I could do it all and do it well. In an effort to maintain my pet status, and the euphoria that came with it, I was willing to work with limited resources, while sacrificing my mental and physical health.

Thomas et al. (2013) first identified the pet to threat syndrome as a common occurrence that ultimately undermines Black women's ability to climb the ladder of success. Findings from Thomas et al. (2013) indicated that Black women are often treated like pets early in their careers. They are adored, cared for, mentored, and supported—usually by White men. This treatment is likened to that of a beloved pet, as long as the behavior of the Black woman is deemed favorable, and the *master* remains in control. When I was appointed to the vice president position, I was completely blinded by the feelings associated with my pet status. I liked being favored, adored, and supported.

After about a year in the vice president position things settled down for me and I was able to devote more time to leadership activities. I found myself exploring new opportunities to implement within the division. As I began to exert my authority and perceived power to institute change, I confronted frequent roadblocks from faculty and administrators. My authority was questioned, as well my expertise regarding the suggested modifications. I was blamed for protecting my employees when in fact I was concerned with enhancing the student experience. When I refused to be dumped on, I was labeled emotional, of passionate or concerned. I was accused of being divisive and had another White male colleague who was also a member of the President's cabinet abruptly hang up the phone on me. My peer, the Vice President of Academic Affairs, who was a White woman, openly chastised me in front of my staff, going so far as to hold up her hand in my face and demand that I stop asking questions and pushing for accountability and change. Both experiences left me feeling extremely angry and discriminated against. It was clear to me that they were empowered to mistreat me by their White privilege and I was expected to just sit and take it. I could not imagine them *ever* openly mistreating a White colleague, regardless of the White colleagues' position, in the manner that they mistreated me.

One of my most enraging experiences that still haunts me to this day demonstrated White privilege, the inability of others to see me (invisibility), and a challenge to the validity of meritocracy—three common experiences noted by African American women in leadership in higher education (Crossman, 2019; Knowles & Lowery, 2012, Stilley, 2021). The college received an opportunity to apply for a grant to open a groundbreaking student support program. This program would provide nonacademic support to students in a variety of ways, including access to food cupboards, crisis resources, housing resources and supplemental nutrition programs. Perfectly aligned to complement the services already available to students, this project would garner a lot of funding and accolades if successfully implemented. I was thrilled that resources were being allocated to student services and I was excited about the additional benefits that our students would soon receive. I waited for further conversations and information. Neither of those came. This nonacademic student support project was given to the Vice President of Academic Affairs—without any hesitation. Certain that the President had made an error, I wrote a memo to him eloquently outlining how the project belonged in student services under my leadership. The President did not even consider making a change.

This experience completely disregarded the organizational structure of the college to accommodate the desires of the dominant race. The separation of duties and responsibilities between the divisions was effectively dismantled by this decision. This was the first and only time that I witnessed such a thing in my 10 years of service in student affairs. The White privilege of the College President and the Vice President of Academic Affairs stole a career enhancing project from me. The dominant race was placed in a position of power, prominence, and influence in a division for which she had no jurisdiction. My dejection was further complicated by my sense of invisibility and lack of merit. Why were my skills and leadership deemed inferior to execute this project? How could my attributes go unseen?

In higher education, structures, beliefs, and values continue to be influenced by the deep-seated characteristics of patriarchy, dominance, and racial and gender bias upon which it was founded (Stilley, 2021). These systemic factors result in racial stratification and are often evident in challenges to the validity of meritocracy (Crossman, 2019; Knowles & Lowery, 2012). Meritocracy suggests that opportunities and advancement are based on one's capabilities, talents, and merits as opposed to one's social status and wealth (Crossman, 2019). White people who champion meritocracy generally consider themselves high in merit (Knowles & Lowery, 2012). Additionally, those engaged in evaluating merit-based practices are influenced by the cultural context of individuals involved (Castilla & Benard, 2010). It seems to me that my cultural context was of great consideration during this evaluation process.

I pushed through and continued to lead the division despite the difficulties that I faced because of my commitment to the students. Seeing students succeed brought me great joy, especially when I could pinpoint an interaction, or program that I facilitated which helped boost their success. I had managed to find ways to cope with the microaggressions and other challenges that resulted from my race and gender. My annual reviews were stellar, and even the President remarked that I could go on to do whatever it was that I desired. My pet status, although waning, was still in tack—until the announcement was made that I had entered a doctoral program. All of a sudden it seemed that I couldn't do much that was right. People complained about everything to everyone, except me.

I wasn't able to make any sense of what happened to me until much later while I was having a conversation with some of my sister-friends. I was working at an institution where the majority of faculty and higher-level administration was not Black. It seems that they could tolerate me as the Vice President of Student Services as long as I was not their "equal." After all, in many institutions' student services is considered second to academic affairs, and without a terminal degree, I was considered "less than" to them also. My lack of a terminal degree was the one thing that they believed would inhibit my further ascension. The attainment of a PhD would certainly open additional doors for me. With increased confidence, abilities and a terminal degree the probability of becoming a college president or THE college president intensified. Like the findings noted in Thomas et al. (2013), my work and talents were being undermined because of a perceived threat to the organizational culture and structure. Within six months from the announcement of my acceptance into a doctoral program my pet status had completely moved to threat status. I was assaulted from every direction. It became apparent that my time at the college was short, and I felt it. I recall sending a friend an email one day during the President's cabinet meeting telling her that I no longer belonged there.

Everlasting Moments

It is very difficult to describe my experiences as a student affairs professional in just one word. In the early stages of my career, I didn't view many of these experiences through a race and gender related lens. Upon reflection, either later the same day, or several weeks later, in the privacy of my thoughts I was able to clearly see the catalyst for the majority of these interactions was a consequence of the intersection of my race and gender.

I considered using words like rewarding, student-centered, difficult, and stereotypical to describe my experiences. I also considered ineffective, race-based, and powerless. All words that are familiar to me and that are referenced in extant research focused on the experiences of African American women in leader in higher education. After careful consideration I landed on the word everlasting. My experiences, especially my leadership experiences in student services are everlasting. Everlasting in the sense that they were continual. As soon as one experience dissipated, another surfaced. Those experiences are everlasting because the resulting emotions cannot be destroyed. Those feelings resurface each time I recount the experience, even though my reaction to them has changed. Everlasting because those experiences have impacted my leadership, career decisions and future as a student affairs administrator in higher education. On very bad days they impact my feelings of self-worth and accomplishments.

Tips and Strategies

Student services is a complicated arena, often conflicted by the desire to support students, and the underfunded, overworked staff, who happen to almost always be mostly African American. To successfully navigate the challenges of working in student affairs it is important to maintain a balance between work and life. In student services, stress comes from relational challenges with coworkers as discussed above, and from helping students cope with their stress and trauma. Self-care and the ability to decompress is vital to one's success in student services. As the challenges are persistent, it is important to be able to relax and reset to maintain one's physical and mental health.

Additionally, it is crucial that you find and develop your circle(s), a group of people that provide much needed support in many different ways. On campus you will need a circle of people who support you. Those that can provide mentorship, honest feedback, advice and prayer. Those that will go to bat with you and for you. Off campus, you will also need a circle. This circle should consist of like-minded individuals that understand the plight of a minority, working in a White dominated industry. This is the circle where you can be free. You can cry, scream, shout, and cuss in this circle. This is the circle that will pick you up and encourage you to keep going and to never give up. Here, in this circle, you will develop strategies and ideas. This is also the circle that will tell you when it is time to leave. And when they tell you it is time to leave, don't be afraid to leave.

I Am Enough

During my time in student affairs I began to affirm "I am enough." It is an affirmation that I continue even now that I no longer work in student affairs. I started saying it daily and put it at the top of my "to do" list. Those three words remind me daily that I was created by God, and He has equipped me with all that I will ever need. Those three words also remind me that despite what others may choose to see, think, or believe, I know that I am enough. I have enough stamina, grace, wit, and talent to overcome any obstacle. I have enough intelligence, strength, fortitude and fire to fulfill all of my wildest dreams. I am enough.

REFERENCES

Baxter-Nuamah, M. (2015). *Through the looking glass: Barriers and coping mechanisms encountered by African American women presidents at predominately white institutions* (3702781) [Doctoral dissertation, Minnesota State University]. Proquest Dissertation and Thesis.

Bowman, N. A. (2011). Promoting participation in a diverse democracy: A meta-analysis of college diversity experiences and civic engagement. *Review of Educational Research, 81*, 29–68. https://doi.org/10.3102/0034543310383047

Braxton, P. (2018). *Brave and fearless: African American women navigating the pathway to a community college presidency* (10824268) [Doctoral dissertation, California Lutheran University]. Proquest Dissertation and Thesis.

Castilla, E. J., & Benard, S. (2010). The paradox of meritocracy in organizations. *Administrative Science Quarterly, 55*(4), 543–576.

Crossman, A. (2019. *Understanding meritocracy from a sociological perspective.* ThoughtCo. https://www.thoughtco.com/meritocracy-definition-3026409

Hylton, D. G. (2012). *In her own voice: A narrative study of the persistence strategies of eight African American women vice presidents for student affairs at predominately white institutions* (3520478) [Doctoral dissertation, Auburn University]. Proquest Dissertations and Theses.

Jones, T. A. (2013). *A phenomenological study of African American women college and university presidents: Their career paths, challenges and barriers* [Dissertation, Capella University]. Minneapolis, Minnesota

Knowles, E. D., & Lowery, B. (2012). Meritocracy, self-concerns, and Whites' denial of racial inequity. *Self and Identity, 11*(2), 202–222.

Levine, A. (1991). The meaning of diversity. *Change, 23*(5), 4–6.

Nevarez, C., & Santamaria, L. J. (2010). *Multicultural/multiethnic education: A critical approach to the educational doctorate in leadership* (Conference proceedings). https://newprairiepress.org/cgi/viewcontent.cgi?article=3718&context=aerc

Schultz, V. (2015). Revisiting *sex*: Gender and sex discrimination fifty years after the Civil Rights Act taking sex discrimination seriously. *Denver University Law Review*.

Stilley, D (2021). *A narrative study of the experiences that disrupt or terminate entry in the community college pipeline for African American women* (28643983) [Doctoral dissertation, Old Dominion University]. Proquest Dissertations and Theses.

Thomas, K. M., Johnson-Bailey, J., Phelps, R. E., Tran, N. M., & Johnson, L. (2013). Moving from pet to threat: Narratives of professional Black women. In L. Comas-Diaz & B. Breene (Eds.), *Psychological health of women of color: Intersections, challenges, and opportunities*. Praeger.

Tienta, M. (2013). Diversity ≠ inclusion: Promoting integration in higher education. *Educational Researcher, 42*, 467–475. https://doi.org/10.3102/0013189X13516164

Tomlin, A. D. (Ed.). (2022). *Working while black: The untold stories of student affairs practitioners.* Information Age Publishing.

Waring, A. (2003). African-American female college presidents: Self-conceptions of leadership. *Journal of Leadership & Organizational Studies, 9*(3). https://doi.org/10.1177/10717919030090030

Wrighten, K. (2018). *Developing a diverse pipeline for community college leadership* (Publication No. 10809935) [Doctoral Dissertation, University of Maryland]. Proquest Dissertations and Theses.

CHAPTER 8

WHAT'S RACISM DOING IN A "NICE" FIELD LIKE STUDENT AFFAIRS?

Counterstories of Those Still Working While Black

Terrell L. Strayhorn

ABSTRACT

Contrary to popular belief, race and racism still matter in America and nowhere is this more obvious than in higher education generally and within student affairs units on college campuses specifically. Though it was understood before, the COVID-19 global pandemic put student affairs professionals on the frontline risking their own safety and well-being for the protection of others. But closer examination of pre- and post-COVID experiences of student affairs staff reveals inequitable racialized patterns of institutional spending on student services, advancement/promotions, and compensation, which align with "the voices" of Black student affairs professionals pushing through crisis management toward a "new normal" where their lives *truly* matter. In this chapter, the author draws on quantitative and qualitative data to argue that race and racism matter, even in a "nice" field like student affairs, and offers advice on how to build workplace, campus conditions where all can thrive and flourish.

Still Working While Black:
The Untold Stories of Student Affairs Practitioners, pp. 69–78
Copyright © 2023 by Information Age Publishing
www.infoagepub.com

INTRODUCTION

Higher education, as an enterprise, in the United States (U.S.) is large, complex, and ever-changing (Thelin, 2004). Its size and capacity is reflected in the enormity of the "system" per se, which is comprised of over 4,300 colleges and universities geographically located across 50 states and territories. Half of these institutions are 2-year community colleges (Levin & Kater, 2013) that educate large shares of first-generation, low-income, and/or underrepresented racial/ethnic minorities (UREMs), some of whom are men of color (e.g., Black, Latinx), Pell-eligible, or military veterans (Wood & Ireland, 2014). Among 4-year institutions, over 260 are research universities, 600+ liberal arts colleges, and 101 are historically Black colleges and universities (HBCUs), federally-designated for the purpose of accommodating the educational needs of African Americans at a time when they were denied admission elsewhere due to the color of their skin (Evans et al., 2002; Strayhorn, 2021a).

The complexity of North American higher education can be observed in several ways. First, institutions vary in size, scope, mission, and control (Altbach et al., 1999). Some minority-serving institutions (MSIs), such as HBCUs and tribal colleges, enroll less than 500 students annually, while other institutions operate multicampus, global systems like Arizona State University, The Ohio State University, and the University of Virginia, my alma mater. Many community colleges are open-access institutions committed *in mission* to providing high-quality, affordable learning options to all who desire postsecondary training, workforce development, and upskilling (Levin & Kater, 2013). While all 2-year community colleges are public institutions, some 2-year institutions are historically Black community colleges (Elliott et al., 2019; Strayhorn, 2022) or tribally controlled (Wright, 1989). Approximately 42% of *all* colleges are private (U.S. Department of Education, 2019).

Another characteristic reflecting the complexity of U.S. higher education is its fairly elaborate division of labor (Hirt et al., 2006). For example, most institutions organize campus work into major divisions or units. Business affairs is comprised of offices engaged in transactional processes, typically including payroll, purchasing, and maintaining an integrated network of financial services (e.g., accounting, internal audits) supporting the broader work of the university (Davidson et al., 2017). Academic affairs, on the other hand, typically refers to the constellation of degree-granting schools/departments, credit-bearing courses/programs, full-time and adjunct faculty, as well as academic and learning supports (e.g., libraries, writing center, honors program), to name a few (Altizer, 1996; Mech, 1997). A third, and significant, sector of the enterprise is *student affairs* referring to an expansive set of programs and services designed to facilitate, nurture, and satisfy the *academic* and *social* needs of student's life; student services range from admissions to advising, counseling and conduct to housing, intramural sports, and orientation, to name a few (Elling, 1997; Sandeen & Barr, 2006).

Though student affairs, as a profession, was established to address the social, emotional (hereafter, "socioemotional"), psychological, and developmental needs of students (Elling, 1997), the field itself is not always so welcoming, nurturing, and supportive for professionals, particularly early career staff (ECS) and administrators of color (AOCs). A steady, and growing, line of research documents that *identity-based inequities* are pervasive and persistent even in a "nice" field like education generally (Johnson & Strayhorn, 2022; Ladson-Billings, 1998) and student affairs specifically.

Without question, race and racism still matter in America and nowhere is this more obvious than when "still working while Black" in student affairs. Although this is not new information, the COVID-19 global pandemic unveiled and exacerbated preexisting inequities (Witham et al., 2015) that put *helping professions* like student affairs, especially ECS and AOCs, on the frontline risking their own safety and well-being for the protection of others (Strayhorn, 2021b, 2021c). Yet, relatively little is known from the published literature about racialized patterns of inequity in student affairs work amid the Great Pandemic—these stories and counterstories (Delgado & Stefancic, 2001) are rarely captured in the extant literature for myriad reasons. This is the gap that the present chapter attempts to fill.

PURPOSE

The purpose of the present chapter is to direct attention to identifying the challenges and opportunities faced by those who are "still working while Black" in student affairs amid the "new normal" set by the COVID crisis. Data from online surveys and one-on-one interviews inform the arguments presented herein. Close examination of pre- and post-COVID experiences of student affairs staff reveals inequitable racialized patterns of institutional spending and support on student services, advancement/promotions, and compensation, which align with "the voices" of Black student affairs professionals pushing through crisis management toward a "new normal" where their lives *truly* matter. Recommendations for future policy, practice, and research are highlighted.

MY STUDENT AFFAIRS STORY

Before diving too far into a general description of the study that serves as a basis for this chapter, it seems important to provide a laconic overview of my own professional trajectory as a way of situating myself within the broader discussion—what qualitative research experts call a *positionality* statement (Denzin & Lincoln, 2000). At the time of this writing, I have worked in higher education for over 20 years as a research analyst, tenure-track/tenured professor, and campus-based academic administrator in progressively responsible positions ranging from program chair and center director to institutional accreditation liaison and chief academic- and student affairs officer (CAO/CSAO), to name a few. Perhaps most relevant to the scope of this chapter, I served successfully for two years as Vice President of Academic and Student Affairs (VPASA) at a private, liberal arts HBCU, overseeing both the academic enterprise (i.e., 5 academic divisions, 34 degree programs, and 100 full-/part-time faculty) and student life (e.g., dean of students, honors, housing, first-year experience).

When I think about *one word* that can be used to describe my experience(s) as a student affairs professional it would be *accountability*. Accountability is an important descriptor of my experiences because, oftentimes, I was expected to address, handle, or resolve issues by virtue of my formal/titular position even *if and when* I was <u>not</u> responsible, directly involved, or present. For instance, once we had a group touring colleges across the state visit our campus. Much to their chagrin, the charter bus they rented overheated and got a flat tire. The 35-plus member group would have to wait several hours for roadside assistance to come fix the problem. Though they visited on their own volition and my workday had long-since ended, I invited them to wait on-campus, helped the facilities crew setup a "waiting room" for them, ordered food and drinks to keep them hydrated, and stayed with them until the situation was rectified and they were back on the road. Though hardly responsible, I certainly felt accountable as the senior student affairs official, chief academic officer, and a physically present "agent" or cultural navigator of the institution (Strayhorn, 2015).

THE STUDY

To help inform the development and direction of this discussion, I conducted an exploratory, mixed methods study examining the experiences of those "still working while Black" in student affairs *after* onset of the COVID-19 pandemic in spring 2020. While full discussion of the study's methods goes well beyond the scope of this brief chapter, suffice it to say the study is part of a larger book project that aims to elicit information from employees in higher education and industry to understand workplace barriers, conditions, and positive outcomes.

Primary data sources include online survey(s) and one-on-one interviews. Survey data were collected using an online tool, developed by the author, consisting of standardized scales (e.g., burnout, intent to leave) and newly constructed scales subjected to pilot testing. Interviews were conducted virtually (via Zoom) by the author using a semi-structured protocol; on average, interviews ranged in length from 30 to 140 minutes. All interviews were transcribed using a professional online service. Survey responses and transcriptions were stored in a password-protected online repository, only available to the principal investigator and authorized members of his graduate research team.

Survey data were analyzed using a mix of appropriate quantitative analytic techniques, while coding methods were used to make sense of interview data. In short, transcripts were read and re-read, marking words and phrases that stood out as possible responses to the core research questions. Codes and categories were sorted and classified to combine those that were related and distinguish those that stood apart. Finally, large codes and categories were compared and contrasted to construct *themes* that seem to capture the essence of participants' experiences "still working while Black" in student affairs. Results are summarized in the next section using basic survey results and verbatim quotes from a few participants, before placing recommendations for future practice, policy, and research.

CHALLENGES IN STUDENT AFFAIRS WORK

Frequent Encounters With Racism and Discrimination. Still today, Black student affairs professionals report encountering racism and discrimination in workplaces. Encounters with racism and discrimination range from racial microaggressions and offensive name-calling to unfair duties/ evaluations and judgments about one's qualifications, to name a few. Microaggressions are defined as "brief and commonplace daily verbal, behavioral, or environmental indignities, whether intentional or unintentional, that communicate hostile, derogatory, or negative racial slights and insults" (Yearwood, 2013, p. 98). In fact, Perez Huber and Solorzano (2015) explain racial microaggressions as a "form of systemic, everyday racism used to keep those at the racial margins in their place" (p. 298). Directed primarily at people of color, racial microaggressions can take many forms: verbal and nonverbal, conscious and unconscious, physically threatening and culturally insensitive, to name a few (Kohli & Solorzano, 2012). Table 8.1 presents a summary of survey results.

Table 8.1

Black Student Affairs Professionals' Encounters With Racism and Discrimination (N = 20)

Incident/Encounter	% Often or Very Often
Hearing/receiving the 'N-word'	70
Dealing with racist stereotypes	75
Unequal treatment based on race	95
Overlooked for opportunity based on race	75
Called to 'speak up' for race	100
Expect to encounter racism at work	90

To help make sense of survey results, one-on-one interviews were structured in a way to elicit relevant examples, insights, and stories from participating Black student affairs professionals. Participants spoke, at length, about their racialized encounters with coworkers, supervisors, and students. Consider the following examples:

> One of my white colleagues said something one day that really gut-punched me. They said: "I wish I was as lucky as you; I mean, I know you work hard but it's like everybody's promoting people of color right now. And I get it, #BlackLivesMatter ... I just wish I could get a little promotion too." It was something like that and I was like ... WTF?! (Jessica, Assistant Vice President)

> Don't get me wrong, there are so many blatant examples but some of that stuff isn't worth talking about because they [white people] know they shouldn't say the "N-word" but it's the little annoying sh*t that pisses me off ... like calling me Tiffany, who is the *only* other Black person in my unit. It's only two of us—you can't get our names right? (Tabitha, Program Specialist)

Participants went on to explain that it's not just the words and comments shared by mostly White coworkers, supervisors, and students that registered as subtle or blatant racial slights, indignities, and offenses, although several agreed that "words matter and words [can] hurt," as Marcus stated. Beyond this, participants explained that "derogatory," "condescending," and "dismissive" comments communicated *in a single moment* combined with past insults and "slick comments" would cascade over time into a series of negative thoughts that left Black student affairs professionals feeling offended, hurt, angry, and, at times, unsafe at work. Those feelings significantly impacted participants' *sense of belonging* at work, compromised their productivity, hijacked their attention, and caused them to feel "out of place" or "othered" in the office. Consequently, many of them reported taking time off from work, missing meetings, or even applying for new jobs or positions as a result.

Surprised to Find It in Student Affairs. Black student affairs professionals in this study almost unanimously agreed that they were "surprised," "disappointed," or "shocked" to find racism, discrimination, and racial microaggressions "so widespread and prevalent in student affairs ... a field that's supposed to be way more inclusive, diverse, and equitable than other professions," as Tasha (financial aid director) explained. In fact, several participants—like Ben (admissions) and Kourtney (student activities)—shared that they choose student affairs as a profession because they expected to be treated fairly, evaluated justly, and embraced warmly by coworkers, supervisors, and students based on what they were taught in graduate school or lived experiences elsewhere.

Experiencing racism, discrimination, and racial microaggressions in student affairs workplaces where they expected to encounter none caused cognitive dissonance for Black student affairs professionals in this pilot study, which resulted in varying responses. For example, racialized stress caused by discrimination and unfair judgments negatively affected their performance and productivity, in several cases. Participants felt isolated and, thus, avoided being in the office, which some referred to as "the site of their oppression" and "injury," to quote informants. Others mentioned working overtime or "going above and beyond" what's required to challenge racist stereotypes spoken by White coworkers (e.g., Blacks are lazy) or to prove others wrong about racial realities. Participants acknowledged the inequity in having to work harder than others, but also worried about the long-term physical, mental, and psychological costs of such burdens.

OPPORTUNITIES IN STUDENT AFFAIRS WORK

Black student affairs professionals' challenges in student affairs work point to several opportunities for the profession generally and campus leaders specifically. First, "College and university campuses, although dedicated to the pursuit of greater knowledge and awareness, are not immune to the influences of racism" (Constantine et al., 2008, p. 49). It's important to note the same is true for person-centered professions like student affairs and those "still working while Black" in student affairs.

Black student affairs professionals in this pilot study reported experiencing routine, everyday exposure to racism, discrimination, and/or racial microaggressions. These were common occurrences, in keeping with dominant theoretical perspectives (Delgado & Stefancic, 2001), that had significant and, at times, seismic impact on staff functioning, team cohesion, and workplace belonging. It is true that isolated events rarely issue much meaning on their own, although that's not always the case—some microaggressions can feel like **MACRO**aggressions [*emphasis added*] in terms of impact. But credible knowledge gained through the counternarratives in this chapter reveals that single incidents compound with other moments (i.e., past, present, and future), avalanching over time into a cascade of negative outcomes: self-deprecating humor, defeatist thought patterns, avoidance behaviors, and thoughts of premature departure or resignation, to name a few.

Experiencing racial stress, trauma, and "injury," as one put it, caused Black student affairs professionals to avoid the office, lose interest in being on campus, or identify other places—"safe spaces"—where they could meet with students, get their work done, or connect with others. Of course this is problematic for a number of reasons, chief among them being that distancing oneself *physically* from departmental peers and spaces may catalyze and encourage *psychological separation*, which leads to premature departure from the position, institution, or profession altogether (Lee & Leonard, 2001).

Consequently, campus leaders, including presidents, provosts, deans, and directors, should view racism, discrimination, and racial microaggressions as major barriers to institutional efforts to foster belonging, improve inclusion, recruit for diversity, or ensure student/staff success. These negative experiences will compromise other large-scale efforts and campaigns, regardless of one's investments. Campus leaders must raise awareness about racial climate; collect, analyze, and report climate data with transparency; and take deliberate actions to eliminate racism, ban discrimination, and address microaggressions. To do this, campus accountability systems must be established or (re)enforced. There must be consequences for individuals and *units* that engage in such behaviors. Taking action to prevent such actions must be matched by efforts to formulate policies and programs that allow those injured by the blows of racism and discrimination to report (even anonymously) through reporting systems that log incidents, locate perpetrators, and lead to sustainable institutional transformation.

It's also true—at least from my experience as a senior-level campus administrator—that one way to address such issues is to reward the behavior(s) one wants repeated. Developing institutional-level systems that offer individual awards, rewards, and designations for fostering welcoming environments, achieving diversity, promoting inclusion and belonging is one effective strategy.

CONCLUSION

Black student affairs professionals' experiences with racism, discrimination, and racial microaggressions is a major concern, whether it captures the attention of campus leaders, professional associations, or not. Information presented in this chapter aims to call these issues to the forefront of campus leaders' minds as they work together to chart a plan for the future of higher education and student affairs amid new norms in a post-pandemic reality where #BlackLivesMatter. Yes, even in a "nice field" like student affairs.

REFERENCES

Altbach, P. G., Berdahl, R. O., & Gumport, P. J. (1999). *American higher education in the twenty-first century: Social, political, and economic challenges.* Johns Hopkins University Press.

Altizer, A. (1996). A model for increasing collaboration between academic and student affairs. *College Student Affairs Journal, 16*(1), 56–61.

Constantine, M. G., Smith, L., Redington, R. M., & Owens, D. (2008). Racial microaggressions against Black counseling and counseling psychology faculty: A central challenge in the multicultural counseling movemenet. *Journal of Counseling & Development, 86,* 348–355.

Davidson, K., McLaren, S., Jenkins, M., Corboy, D., Gibbs, P. M., & Molloy, M. (2017). Internalized homonegativity, sense of belonging, and depressive symptoms among Australian Gay men. *J Homosex, 64*(4), 450–465. https://doi.org/10.1080/00918369.2016.1190215

Delgado, R., & Stefancic, J. (2001). *Critical race theory: An introduction.* New York University Press.

Denzin, N. K., & Lincoln, Y. S. (2000). The discipline and practice of qualitative research. In N. K. Denzin & Y. S. Lincoln (Eds.), *Handbook of qualitative research* (2nd ed., pp. 1-29). SAGE.

Elling, T. (1997). *Nature and purpose of the division of student affairs.* University of North Carolina-Charlotte. Retrieved April 12, from http://www.uncc.edu/stuaffairs/purpose.html

Elliott, K. C., Warshaw, J. B., & deGregory, C. A. (2019). Historically Black community colleges: A descriptive profile and call for context-based future research. *Community College Journal of Research & Practice, 43*(10-11), 770–784.

Evans, A. L., Evans, V., & Evans, A. M. (2002). Historically Black colleges and universities (HBCUs). *Education, 123*(1), 3–16, 180.

Hirt, J. B., Bennett, B. R., Strayhorn, T. L., & Amelink, C. A. (2006). What really matters? The nature of rewards for student affairs administrators at historically Black colleges and universities. *NASAP Journal, 9*(1), 83–99.

Johnson, R. M., & Strayhorn, T. L. (2022). Examining race and racism in Black men doctoral student socialization: A critical race mixed methods analysis. *Journal of Diversity in Higher Education.* https://doi.org/https://doi.org/10.1037/dhe0000420

Kohli, R., & Solorzano, D. G. (2012). Teachers, please learn our names! Racial microaggressions and the K–12 classroom. *Race, Ethnicity, & Education, 15*(4), 441–462. https://doi.org/https://doi.org/10.1080/13613324.2012.674026

Ladson-Billings, G. (1998). Just what is critical race theory and what's it doing in a *nice* field like education? *Qualitative Studies in Education, 11*(1), 7–24.

Lee, L. J., & Leonard, C. A. (2001). Violence in predominantly White institutions of higher education: Tenure and victim blaming. *Journal of Human Behavior in the Social Environment, 3,* 167–186.

Levin, J. S., & Kater, S. (Eds.). (2013). *Understanding community colleges.* Routledge.

Mech, T. F. (1997). The managerial roles of chief academic officers. *Journal of Higher Education, 68,* 282–298.

Perez Huber, L., & Solorzano, D. G. (2015). Racial microaggressions as a tool for critical race research. *Race, Ethnicity, & Education, 18,* 297–320.

Sandeen, A., & Barr, M. J. (2006). *Critical issues for student affairs: Challenges and opportunities.* Jossey-Bass.

Strayhorn, T. L. (2015). Reframing Academic Advising for Student Success: From Advisor to Cultural Navigator. *NACADA Journal, 35*(1), 56–63. https://doi.org/10.12930/nacada-14-199

Strayhorn, T. L. (2021a). *A pledge of allegiance to America's historically Black colleges and universities: Key priorities of the Biden-Harris education agenda.* Center for the Study of HBCUs, Virginia Union University.

Strayhorn, T. L. (2021b). Achieving racial equity in oral health among distressed populations amid COVID-19. *International Journal on Infectious Disease & Epidemiology, 2*(1), 9–10. https://doi.org/https://doi.org/10.51626/ijide.2021.02.00003

Strayhorn, T. L. (2021c). Investigating the impact of COVID-19 on basic needs security among vulnerable college students: An exploratory study. *Academia Letters,* Article 1786. https://doi.org/https://doi.org/10.20935/AL1786

Strayhorn, T. L. (2022). Lessons learned from institutional responses to COVID-19: Evidence-based insights from a qualitative study of historically Black community colleges. *Community College Journal of Research & Practice, 46*(1–2), 30–40. https://doi.org/https://doi.org/10.1080/10668926.2021.1975173

Thelin, J. R. (2004). *A history of American higher education.* Johns Hopkins University Press.

U.S. Department of Education. (2019). *The condition of education 2018.*

Witham, K., Malcom-Piqueux, L., Dowd, A. C., & Bensimon, E. M. (2015). *America's unmet promise: The imperative for equity in higher education.* Assocition of American Colleges and Universities.

Wood, J. L., & Ireland, S. M. (2014). Supporting Black male community college success: Determinants of faculty-student engagement. *Community College Journal of Research & Practice, 38*(2–3), 154–165. https://doi.org/10.1080/10668926.2014.851957

Wright, B. (1989). Tribally controlled community colleges: An assessment of student satisfaction. *Community College Journal of Research & Practice, 13*(2), 119–128.

Yearwood, E. L. (2013). Microaggression. *Journal of Child & Adolescent Psychiatric Nursing, 26*(1), 98–99. https://doi.org/https://doi.org/10.1111/jcap.12021

SECTION III

YOU GON' GET ME: ALL OF ME!

CHAPTER 9

NO REAL N****S ALLOWED

Palatable Black Masculine Performance in Student Affairs

Nathan A. Stephens, Jamarco Clark, and Dyrell Ashley

INTRODUCTION

This chapter is written as a collaborative autoethnography (CAE) based on our perspectives as Black men with experience in the field of student affairs. Chang et al. (2013) defines CAE as an autoethnography written by two or more authors. Through this chapter readers will notice that our experiences are simultaneously similar and different. As Black men we are not a monolithic group despite the racial stereotypes and racialized tropes that fail to differentiate us. However, we do have group and individual identities that merge and diverge such as violating what is deemed as palatable Black masculine performance in student affairs. The three authors of this chapter are connected through their experiences as Black men in student affairs and as members of Alpha Phi Alpha Fraternity Incorporated.

WHO WE ARE

Nathan: I have 14 years of experience in student affairs where I worked at predominately White institutions in the Midwest. My career includes serving as a Senior Coordinator of a Black culture center for 7.5 years, Director of center with a Black, Latinx, Women, and LGBTQ+ units for

3 years, and Director of another Black Cultural Center for 3.5 years. The institutions include two state flagship institutions and 1 regional institution.

Jamarco: I have over 8 years of experience at predominately White institutions in the Midwest. These institutions include a small-private institution, a community college, a regional institution, and a large public flagship institution. His experience in student affairs includes serving as a Hall Director and Area Coordinator in Residential Life, as a Coordinator and Director in Volunteerism and Service Learning, Director of Student Life, Director of Leadership and Engagement, and as an Assistant Dean and Director of Leadership and Engagement.

Dyrell: I have over 3 years of experience in student affairs where he worked at historically White institutions in the Midwest and Historically Black Colleges in the South. My career includes serving as an Admissions Counselor, Assistant Business Operations Manager of a Multicultural Center, Antiracist/DEI Coordinator, Project Manager of DEI practices, Antiracist/DEI Consultant, and Interim Associate Director for the Office of Diversity and Inclusion. The institutions include a 4-year public historically White Institution (HWI), 4-year small, private liberal arts HWI, and 2 small private liberal arts Historically Black Colleges and Universities (HBCUs).

Each of the authors will now provide their individual responses to prompts that helped to solicit their experiences in student affairs.

FROM THE PROJECTS TO A PhD
BUT THEY STILL CAN'T SEE ME

One Word Description of Student Affairs' Experience

Volatile is the word that I would use. The Oxford Dictionary (n.d.) includes within its definition of volatile "liable to change rapidly and unpredictably, especially for the worse."

This word was chosen because that has been my experience and because of the politics on each of the campuses that I have worked. The politics have been racial where they manifested as a product of campus climate and economics. The economic aspect is related to my experiences in diversity or multicultural student affairs. Because cultural centers, multicultural student affairs, and diversity initiatives are "add-ons" historically to predominately White institutions, my experience has been that they are inevitably viewed for budget reductions during lean fiscal times. But the politics and challenges have also been intracultural, mostly related to legacies and resistance to change. Finally, the politics are almost always connected to changes in leadership that occurs within senior leaders such as Chancellors, Presidents, or Vice Presidents, as well as the department level. It is frustrating, but it is what it is for now at least.

Challenges of Race and Gender

Challenges of race and gender were experienced through the campus and local political climates. It felt as though Black males who were deemed nonthreatening by White administrators and, administrators of color who were supportive of maintaining the status quo, were palatable. As a Black man in student affairs who voiced my opinions, I soon began experiencing negative performance reviews. But the pinnacle was being told by my White male supervisor that some of my "colleagues were afraid of me." This sentiment really upset me because it is based on racist tropes and stereotypes that date back to the establishment of the Ku Klux Klan (KKK). This group allegedly came into existence to protect White women from Black men.

Opportunities

One of the biggest opportunities that I experienced due to race and gender stems from me cocreating the Mizzou Black Men's Initiative (MBMI) in 2009. The year before I observed that Black male collegians were not engaging in Black student organizations on campus. The organizations were led almost solely by Black women and as an advisor to some of these organizations, the absence of Black men was obvious.

A few years before this, I became certified to do rape and sexual assault training with male athletic teams. I was approached primarily because I was a Black male who stood 6'1, 215 pounds that could walk into a room full of college athletes with credibility. During one of the trainings, I became acquainted with a young man who would become my graduate assistant a short time later and cocreator of the MBMI alongside me. Ultimately, the work with athletes I believe occurred because I was a Black man. And that work led to the creation of MBMI and opportunities to do presentations about the MBMI program at conferences and sit on panels about BMIs and men of color initiatives.

Strategies and Tips for Navigating Student Affairs

I would say that to navigate student affairs, one should be specific and explicit about their aims for being in the profession. Create a career plan that includes the opinions and input of allies and coconspirators that you have cultivated and thoroughly evaluated to assist with your journey. Furthermore, be intentional about thinking outside of the proverbial box about who your allies will be. My entrance into student affairs came through the support of a White administrator whom I met when I was his janitor while finishing my bachelor's degree. Finally, it is essential to know and have explored "who you are." Specifically, what are your values, beliefs, assumptions, fears, hopes, dreams, and so on? And how do these things guide your decision making related to your career and professional maneuvers? Knowing who you are and how you prioritize the multiple aspects of selfhood can help you if you are face to face with potentially life changing.

Words of Affirmation

"You are enough." Student affairs can be a thankless job with workdays that often extend into the evenings and weekends. Students, coworkers, administrators may not always see or acknowledge your good works. Fight the internal battle that may occur within you that causes you to question your own worth simply because others do not see it. My grandmother once told me that sometimes you may be the only light in a room full of darkness. This is an incredibly difficult position to be in because human beings are communal by nature, and all humans like to be "liked," accepted, and respected. Choose your battles wisely and do not feel compelled to fight every fight.

What Else Does the World Need to Know About Me as a Black Student Affairs Professional?

It is my belief that Black men who aspire to work in student affairs, must be aware that anti-Black misandry manifests against certain Black masculine performances. The "Real Nigga" Black masculine performance does not bode well in student affairs. Some historical racial tropes are described by Tyree et al. (2008) with the toms defined as "good Negroes who are loyal to their White masters;" the coons are the "no account Negroes who are lazy and subhuman;" the tragic mulatto is the "mixed race person with a divided racial heritage," and the buck "who was big, strong, hypersexual, and stupid" (p. 469). However, a manifestation of Black masculine performance from these authors is "the real nigga." The real nigga is often spoken of in hip-hop music and is embodied by the late Tupac Shakur. Tupac's (1991) intelligence, complexity, commitment to Blackness, street cred, and authenticity is what merits this designation. A quick example is found in his song *Violent*, where he raps about the word "nigga," as an acronym meaning "never ignorant getting goals accomplished."

Often absent in discussions about Black men's masculine performances in scholarly literature is a description of it as authentic Blackness that is unapologetically culturally rooted. While this mindset is often viewed as valuable in urban Black communities with street codes that influence how Black men where Black people are "from the streets," and live their lives with a high amount of self-determinism and are unapologetic about their truths. The real nigga remains connected to the communities that he emanates from and defies assimilationist values. This assimilation process Tierney (1999) calls "cultural suicide" is what Black collegians must do to become fully enmeshed into the White middle-class values and norms of higher education. Black men entering the field of student affairs may have to grapple with this decision to commit "cultural suicide." Early in my career, a Black male mentor sterned warned me, "man you can't be brining that Malcolm X shit up in here." No real n****s allowed! That would include you too Malcolm X!

FROM THE 'HOODS OF PENSACOLA TO THE HOODS OF THE ACADEMY

One Word

Opportunity! Opportunities have come in great abundance as my career in student affairs has unfolded. Since 2014 I have had the opportunity to work at five different institutions. Two small private liberal arts, one community college, one public regional selective, and public research one institution. When most people hear that someone has been in the profession for only nine years and has worked at five different institutions, I am certain red flags begin to fly (I have seen it happen in interview processes). However, I always caution individuals to look deeper than what they see on the resume. Like the word that has defined my career, I credit the ability to have worked at those five different institutions to the opportunities that have been presented to me. I always question if the opportunities are present because I am a Black man, or is it because people appreciate the work I have been able to do. While I will never fully know the answer, those two things coupled together have been vital in my career navigation and will always likely play a role whether overt or covert.

Challenges of Race and Gender

In my experiences, I have not encountered many negative challenges of being a Black man working in student affairs. For the most part, the greatest challenges have come in my work as a front-line responder to students going through traumatic experiences while on campus. Given my background in student affairs functional areas such as residence life, student conduct, and Title IX, I have been afforded many opportunities to work with students through some of the toughest periods/times of their lives. While many times it was a joy being able to assist students in overcoming these challenges, there were few when the aftermath of assisting the students was challenging for my own well-being as a Black male student affairs professional. I specifically think about the many situations where I have worked with students through suicidal ideation, while it is great to help the student get to a point of no longer considering causing harm to themselves—the lasting impact after working with those situations often left me feeling unwell. When met with these challenges, like most Black people who do this work—I often "bottled up" my emotions to ensure I was continuing to support the students. While this is not the best practice for Black professionals, it has become the norm. In a recent study on Black men student affairs professionals, Clark (2022) found that when national incidents like George Floyd, Breonna Taylor, and Ahmad Arbery take place, Black men student affairs professional are some of the first called upon for campuses responses. Furthermore, they are oft-times sidestepping the raw emotions they may be feeling because of the incidents, simply because they have been conditioned as Black men in student affairs to put their emotions to the side and tend to those of the students. For years, Black men in student affairs will have come to the aid of the students we support, even if it means delaying the impacts the incidents or establishing understanding of how they affect us.

Opportunities

Any challenges that I have experienced are offset by the opportunities that I spoke about earlier. Opportunity has truly been the key for me. While I am not one to want to be tokenized and hope that I have made it this far in my career on the merits of my work and not my race—I do understand and acknowledge that sometimes you receive an opportunity because of it. You may be put in the position because of you race—and at that point it is all about how you expend the agency afforded to you. Throughout my career there have been several instances where my identity as a Black man has served me well. I particularly think to the times when I have been able to work with Black male students who come from similar less than ideal upbringings. In these situations, I am fortunate to be able to be living proof what an education can do for someone who has the cards stacked against them at birth. While this is just one access point to connecting with

Black male students, it is one that has been the most genuine and has led to fruitful discussion and lifelong bonds with former Black male students.

Strategies and Tips for Navigating Student Affairs

Play the game to the best of your ability. In my terms, "the game" in student affairs is the politics. Many will share that they have no interest in playing politics. Again, I say, play it to the best of your ability. The presence of politics is inevitable in student affairs, no matter the institution type or location. Having said that, understanding how to strategically navigate the politics that exist within your institution will not only allow you to see through a big picture lens, but it will also allow you to tap into networks when you need them the most. The networks will help you to understand how to navigate strategically and selectively. Playing the game should not be confused with selling out [i.e., going against your morals, compromising your integrity]. On the contrary, view it as an opportunity to establish and obtain agency to support your work and the students you are tasked with supporting.

Also, get a mentor. While selecting a mentor is important, selecting one who understands you is even more important. In my opinion a mentor is someone who will offer you support, but also challenge your thinking. When selecting a mentor, it is important to be intentional as bad advice from a mentor could lead to the demise of a career. Also understand that you do not have to take all the advice given from the mentor. Furthermore, I recommend having a mentor that is housed on your campus (if possible) and another that is outside of campus. Being able to discuss campus culture with these two different mentors will provide different, yet beneficial outcomes.

Words of Affirmation

"Why not me" The three words why not me, have allowed me to achieve, accomplish, and attempt many feats within student affairs. Understanding that for everything that must be done within student affairs, someone must do it. So, I often ask myself, "why not me?" Someone must be a college or university president someday, why not me? Someone must defy odds and be a first-generation doctoral graduate, why not me? Someone must knock down every barrier placed before them, why not me? The mindset of why not me? is not one of entitlement, yet one of fearless empowerment to go after all the things one desires for themselves whether professionally or personally. Thus far, this mindset has led to me being an Assistant Dean of

Students and Doctor of Education at the age of 29. And I am confident that with the proper preparation and hard work, the "why not me?" mindset will lead me to accomplish my career goal of one day becoming a College or University President. So, the question I leave you with is, why not me? And why not you?

What Else Does the World Need to Know About Me as a Black Student Affairs Professional (BSAPro)?

As a BSAPro, it is important to note that although I am committed to doing my best to care for the students, I also matter. Many times, BSAPro are tasked with being first responders for many issues that face students of colors (and others) on their respective campuses. With that, many of these instances tend to have a resounding impact on the BSAPro as well. Unfortunate, due to our responsibility to provide guidance and care for the students, we [BSAPro] are not afforded the opportunity to bask in what these issues/experiences mean for us. Lastly, the world must know that we are here, we will continue to give care to our students, but we would like some care, too!

Through Adversity, I Still Rise

One Word

The one word that I would use to describe my experience in student affairs is resistant. I choose this word because as a young Black male in student affairs, I wanted to enact changes that I felt would be positive. But politics, power dynamics, and hegemony made it hard to create change. Also, in many instances, my recommendations were not considered. I attribute this to power dynamics and my status in the hierarchy. In some of the institutions I have worked at, many ideas and initiatives were not valued or taken seriously unless it was from individuals with the titles of Director or Associate Director. These individuals oftentimes passively listened to my ideas, but then would not try to enact them. I even caught individuals who were my superiors talking behind my back saying things like "who do he think he is" or "He act like he run this show and he don't." I was baffled by these comments because I was trying to accomplish our mission and keep students in the center, but because of my title and demographics, they turned my good intentions into an unnecessary competition. I quickly learned that individuals in higher education will be resistant to new ideas if they feel that it challenges one's authority.

Challenges

Oftentimes, my race and gender came with the challenge of my voice not being brought to the table. Also, I found myself having to overexplain changes that I would want to make or even new programs that I wanted to implement. I also faced a lot of resistance from administration on new diversity initiatives and program to the point where it started to become silencing. I remember when I began a role during my master's degree program, I worked with individuals with similar demographics to myself, but I was the only Black male "subordinate." The Director, a Black woman whom I was excited to work with, would constantly turn down any of my ideas without any explanation. I remember her constant questioning and criticisms to any of my programming or initiatives even though they were presented with no errors. I started to notice this pattern, but she would not act in the same fashion to my female counterparts of different demographic makeup who did not produce the same level of work. I started feeling like I was constantly hitting a brick wall because I was told my ideas would be valued, but they were not. It started to make me less excited for my work because I was constantly being blocked, so naturally I had to find a way around this system. Once I seen that I was beginning to speak less in meetings, stop my ideas, and not like what I was doing, I knew I needed to make a change. With any program I was over, I had to ensure key stakeholders were present to see my work and its importance I order to reclaim my voice. There was even more obstacles place to the point where it caused extreme fatigue. There comes a time where one is tired of constantly fighting to be heard. Once I noticed how I was being treated differently, I knew I had to play the game. I ensured that I began documenting any inequities in the department. I also began documenting and blind copying key institutional stakeholders, so they were aware of my work and to be protected if any retaliation was taken against me.

Opportunities

Being a Black man specializing in diversity, equity, and inclusion (DEI) practices has opened some doors for me. There are more institutions and offices wanting a consultant to aid in the reformation of their historically White or DEI deficit spaces. These opportunities were good for institutions who truly wanted to change. It also expanded opportunities for me to implement new trainings and programming that those institutions did not think about otherwise. I began to become a respected DEI trainer among not only my institution, other higher education, and business institutions. This experience reclaimed my confidence as a Black male practitioner. Coning from not having a favorable experience in higher education and being silenced, I had to keep fighting to make my mark. These experiences showed me that I can persist through all adversities as well as situate myself as an expert in the field. This taught me that as a Black man my fight is eternal, but I am enough regardless of those who try to me down.

Strategies and Tips for Navigating Student Affairs

Some tips that I have found helpful to navigate the realm of student affairs is first stay grounded in who I am. By this, I mean, I am intentional about not getting lost in the politics and forgetting my own morals, ethics, and values. Additionally, I encourage folks to keep up with meditating, working out, spiritual practices, or any other hobby and spiritual practices that will help disconnect from the fatigue and stay charged. Another piece of advice that I would give is to know the system in which you work and beyond. The world of student affairs is very small. Specifically, be careful with who and what you speak about and to who. Every coworker is not going to have your best interest at heart, and some will even view you as competition. It is important for you to know your allies and keep records of your intellectual property. Moreover, take advantage of opportunities and become knowledgeable in multiple areas. It is beneficial for you to know how the different systems work and are intertwined to help you build sound arguments, programming, and change policy/procedure.

Words of Affirmation

My main mantra that I live by especially in this profession is "He who has not faced adversity, doesn't know their true strength." This has been stored in my memory since I was young. Anytime my work gets taxing or things get rough, I think about this quote, and it shows me that I am being pushed to be stronger than I thought I was. The more challenges one faces, the stronger one becomes for overcoming it. This quote has helped mold me into the man, mentor, and professional I am today.

CONCLUSION

In summary, this chapter shared some of the experiences of three Black men with experience in the field of student affairs. We acknowledge the multidimensional and vast experiences that Black men. However, we also acknowledge that some of the themes that emerged from the narratives in this chapter are the impact of the political climate and campus politics on the experiences of Black men in this field. Second, the authors shared about being silenced or having their voices muted in some capacity. Next was the theme of "struggle" that appeared as various types of resistance, barriers, or having to fight in some capacity. Finally, there was a consensus in the narratives that the primary motivation for doing this work in student affairs, was the authors' love of students. Black men who aspire to have a career in student affairs must prepare mentally and emotionally to contend with some sort of politics, labor to maintain voice, and know that the proverbial "struggle" is real. But these experiences often are eroded when you see students that you have supported in a myriad of ways, walk across the stage and graduate.

REFERENCES

Chang, H., Ngunjiri, F. W., & Hernandez, K. C. (2013). *Collaborative autoethnography.* Walnut Left Coast Press.

Clark, J. (2022). *"Where is the support?": Black men student affairs professionals' experience with secondary trauma* (Order No. 30248221). Available from ProQuest Dissertations & Theses Global (2771684124). http://login.proxy.lib. uiowa.edu/login?url=https://www.proquest.com/dissertations-theses/where-is-support-black-men-student-affairs/docview/2771684124/se-2

Oxford Dictionary. (n.d.). Volatile. In *Oxford Dictionary.* https://www. oxfordlearnersdictionaries.com/us/definition/english/volatile#:~:text=volatile-,adjective,a%20highly%20volatile%20personality

Shakur, T. (1991). Violent (Song). *On 2Pacalypse Now.* Interscope; Universal.

Tierney, W. G. (1999). Models of minority college-going and retention: Cultural integrity versus cultural suicide, *The Journal of Negro Education, 68*(1), 80–91. https://www.jstor.org/stable/2668211

Tyree, T. C. M., Byerly, C. M., & Hamilton, K. A. (2011). Representations of (new) Black masculinity: A news-making case study. *Journalism, 13*(4), 467–482. https://doi.org/10.1177/1464884911421695

CHAPTER 10

DR. MRS. MOM

The Power of an Integrated Life

Michelle A. Nelson and Caryn Reed-Hendon

ABSTRACT

In this chapter, we seek to provide a viewpoint for many Black women who had to pivot in their careers to remain relevant, present and successful while also having to manage other responsibilities. Strengthened by the social-cultural norms of marriage and family, we were able to incorporate the relevance of our identities such as Black feminist thought with our own lived experience as Dr. Mrs. Mom in student affairs. This chapter outlines individual and collective lessons learned and strategies of our own lived experiences with the hope that the reader will not put off life, or minimize their own desires, but to consider an integrated life that fosters balance.

INTRODUCTION

We Are Here to Be an Example

We do not hesitate to share with others our lived experiences as Black women in student affairs. Our lives serve as footprints for others to follow as well as a testimony to our resilience. This chapter describes two women's stories in the quest of "having it all." Also, in the recognition of doing so, requires sacrifice and a reframing of what "it" and "all" means in the context of a lived experience. Reflecting introspectively on the multiple

Still Working While Black:
The Untold Stories of Student Affairs Practitioners, pp. 93–104
Copyright © 2023 by Information Age Publishing
www.infoagepub.com

pathways to Dr. Mrs. and Mom, while not necessarily always in this order, begs the question of why reframing and context matter?

HOW THE EARLY YEARS SHAPED US

Our lived experiences help us to offer a unique perspective to the student affairs profession by first sharing how our lives were shaped in our childhood. These early years have helped to shape our identities and how we view our careers. Our brief stories bring context and evidence that have shaped us in the student affairs profession, adding value to our individual approaches to the work and personality in how we engage with our community.

My Name Is Michelle

A friend once shared an Arabic proverb, "The first step toward success is not to be a prisoner of the conditions that you were born in." I am the product whose social and environmental factors did not define my future. My childhood was plagued with poverty, drugs, alcohol and abuse. According to societal norms, I should have found myself in a cycle of generational curses and my dreams not even actualized. It was my mother and God, her tenacity and perseverance to change and overcome in order to save her children from the vicious cycle. It was my mother who first introduced me to higher education and demanded educational excellence. Regardless of their past, both of my parents overcame their own life struggles and celebrated with me as the first in my family to earn a doctorate.

My Name Is Caryn

I come from a family of competing dichotomies. Education was pushed on my sibling and I as the key that would unlock the door to many opportunities in life. There was also a misogynistic attitude towards the girls in our family; boys will be boys and girls need to learn to take care of themselves and others. I always knew I would get a college degree; I claimed it at the age of 7 after reading the *World Book Encyclopedia*. My dad thought it was cute, my mom was determined to not let that dream die. The older I got, the more my relationship status became discussion fodder for family gatherings. My maternal grandmother used to tell my girl cousins and I, "A man does not want a woman smarter than him. Get any smarter we will have to buy you a husband." I always took offense to that notion, but now as a divorced, co-parenting woman in my 40s there's a part of me that wonders if she was right.

SOCIETAL EXPECTATIONS:
THE MULTIPLE DIMENSIONS OF WOMANHOOD

First, let us preface that the multiple dimensions of womanhood we speak about are not meant to exclude or to minimize others; however, we speak about societal expectations that have framed our own lived experiences and interpretations. It was once considered that during the coming of age in a young girl's life was met with gender-normative roles and relationship expectations. These expectations perpetuated the notion that a girl only needed to be outfitted with enough education to care for a husband, family, and home. To account for historical social expectations and educational policy reforms, Eisenmann (2007) summarized that

> Turning an historical lens on women's education helps demonstrate that discrimination against them—sometimes overt and other times quite unawares—has led to limited expectations for where, how, and why women should participate in education ... the belief that they should be educated ... matching their future roles as wives and mothers excluded them at times when domestic concerns prevailed. (p. 12)

The rites of passage for womanhood has been synonymous with the roles of wife and mother; however, as women of color, specifically Black women, our historical narrative has not much allowed for this rite of passage but to be in servitude. We argue against this standard because of its roots in patriarchy and White supremacy. Therefore, it is important for us to recognize and dismantle gender-normative roles and expectations.

Throughout adulthood the societal standard of what womanhood has been, including but not limited to, being partnered, becoming a parent, and other hallmarks, also brought forth the "struggle to juggle" dilemma. Henderson (2006) described the conflict as one that is ongoing and significantly impacts a woman's health, relationships, work performance, and at times results in the decrease of satisfaction in their work and personal lives. Recognizing the need to resist such intersecting oppressions, particularly if there is hesitancy toward gendered expectations, it is imperative to be increasingly empowered to speak about the consciousness of women and their multiple roles in the workplace and personal lives.

The Competing Narrative

Michelle. It is often said that for women to advance the professional ladder, some things have to wait. Perhaps I took it literally. My desire to have it all was often placed within calculated milestones for degree attainment and career trajectory. I thought I needed to sacrifice love, family, and myself to fit in professionally. Over the years, I attempted to be the best, almost too perfect, to ascertain the lifestyle and set accomplishments that were expected of me. I was single and living my best life. I started my PhD studies in 2013. I knew it would take me approximately five years to complete. It was not until after a failed marriage (when I was younger), and a failed relationship that I knew that my "timeclock" to meet my other needs was approaching. Although I knew women who were getting married later in life, having children at later ages; what was not in my favor were the medical conditions that I thought would prevent me from having children. As I got older, the men I dated often already had medical procedures to prevent additional children because they started their families in their young 20s and no longer wanted more. Yet, I held on to the hope that I would love again despite my perception that time was running out. My identity is based on my positionality and intersection of my social-cultural norms. I am an African American, spiritual, heterosexual, divorcee, overcomer of many life battles, and now a woman in my 40s, I am a wife and mother of two; I find my multiple identities intersecting and responding to my intellectual, professional, and personal paths sometimes in congruence and other times in denial.

Caryn. While in my master's degree program two close friends were getting married a week apart. I stood in both weddings as maid of honor for one and bridesmaid for the other. For those two weeks I felt badgered about my marital status by anyone that learned that I wasn't in a relationship. It was at the second wedding where I met Marlon [pseudonym] and I felt caught in a conundrum after meeting him because I was a few weeks away from attending a summer out-of-state internship. We spent the summer emailing and calling each other, it was nice. When I returned from my internship, we ended up dating over the course of completing my degree. Six months to the date after earning my master's degree and being in a new job, we were engaged. While colleagues and loved ones were happy for me, I felt the need to work harder to prove my dedication as if I wasn't getting married. The overcompensation led to worry that consumed me. Open time in my schedule was often scarce and rarely did I take time away because I didn't think that I would be believed for my need to do so. We married a year and a half later and didn't go on honeymoon, there was no time.

Multiple Pathways to Dr. Mrs. Mom

Michelle. It was the year 2017 when I met my husband online. I was very fortunate, he had never been married, no children, and had a very successful business. For me, online dating was a success. I put myself out there and before I knew it I was engaged 11 months later. It was the year 2018, I did not know but my life entered into a season of transition. For the first time in my life, I underwent medical procedures, my job was eliminated, and I was one chapter away from completing my PhD. In October 2018, I defended my dissertation, married my husband, and had a honeymoon baby by December 2018. These are my truths.

Caryn. After a couple of years married, I felt stagnated in my role because I wanted to do more to support students. By then, I'd contemplated getting a doctorate, it was the right time to go for it. Around the same time, my spouse began to ask about expanding our family. Nothing about our relationship at that point said we were remotely ready to have a child. While mildly supportive of my going back to school, he decided to earn an MBA and MA in engineering. Thankfully, the family planning discussion was tabled because we were both now in demanding academic programs.

When I started my studies, it was said to my cohort that completing the program was entirely within our control and not to make any big changes in our lives that would impede our progress, such as getting married, getting divorced, having a baby, buying a house, getting a new position, or any other high stress life experiences. One by one, members of my cohort had big life changes, myself included. We worked very hard to keep one another accountable and sought support from our department chair, dissertation committees, and others to stay on the path to completion. One by one, we completed our dissertations and celebrated with each other as we passed our defenses, anxiously awaiting graduation day. The same day I passed my defense, my spouse and I had a very tense conversation again about becoming a family of three. I felt ready to expand my career, ready to do research, not become a mother just yet. I wanted to enjoy being "PhD." Three months later, I was pregnant.

We Identify as Black Feminists

Black feminist thought (BFT) is a theory and analytical framework that provides women the tools to practice intellectual activism as a means to take back the power and resist intersecting oppressions (Collins, 2000). This dimension we speak about is the empowerment and consciousness of women. As Black women in student affairs, we embrace the responsibility to listen to and advocate for marginalized voices that have been historically ignored while navigating the realities of multiple viewpoints within a White-dominant power structure. We openly discuss systematic inequity from multiple and intersecting perspectives and by doing so, as Black feminists, we are empowered to name the systems of inequality, vocalize it, and dismantle them in our practice.

THE STUDENT AFFAIRS PROFESSION

The work of student affairs can be defined as a critical administrator responsible for cultivating an environment that is both challenging and supporting, advocating for, and managing to ensure all students feel that they belong. Student affairs professionals are often described as the non-instructional staff, responsible for the affairs outside the classroom while attempting to fix and respond to the ever-changing needs of the student (Duggan, 2008; Jones & Taylor, 2013). According to Student Affairs Administrators in Higher Education, student affairs professionals "promote student learning and development" (naspa.org). For more information about the work of student affairs, one should consider the professional associations such as NASPA or foundational documents such as the CAS standards or the NASPA Professional Competency Areas for Student Affairs Educators (naspa.org).

Cast Your Net Wide

In our professional experience, we have learned to cast our professional net wide, hoping that they go deep enough for our work to stand out loud enough and to be recognized as leading experts. In addition, as professionals we are burdened with the mindset of blending in to advance far enough in our careers to be effective, seeking to stand out and be welcomed in our workplaces, with the contrast of fear or rejection from so-called "doing too much."

Michelle. The best way to describe my career path thus far has been focused and broad. I was very fortunate to enter into higher education as a work study student. I earned a liberal arts degree in political science and French. Professionally, I started working in student affairs after graduation during the year 2002. Even though my undergraduate degree did not have a clear career pathway into higher education, it provided me with a broad transferable skill set that supported my academic direction to earn a MBA in strategic management before earning my PhD in education leadership. I have progressively worked in student affairs, housing, student life, academic advising, career, and education advising, financial aid, international student advising, study abroad, student success, research and teaching. My highest career position obtained was when I served as the Assistant Provost for Student and Global Affairs. Reflecting from the many positions held, I have had to lean in by strengthening my skills as a collaborator, as well as being able to bring teams together across institutional divisions and departments.

Caryn. I've often said that people don't choose higher education or student affairs as a career choice, the career chooses us. I completed my communication studies bachelor's degree at the turn of the century and landed in a research university in the Dean of Students office running Orientation for a couple of years, then financial aid for a year, and finally in the McNair Scholars/TRiO programs. In my time there, I was mentored by seasoned student affairs and academic affairs professionals, taking the advice and support to start my master's degree in a very strong higher education student affairs program. Every opportunity to learn more about the university and how it works, I took on, being fascinated at the operation and the connectedness to the surrounding community. Over the course of completing my degree, I considered moving out of state due to opportunities being limited in the area. In a last-ditch effort, I applied for and landed an entry level Assistant Director position in Admissions and Orientation at another institution. I stayed in that position for five years working towards an opportunity for advancement. When I asked, I was immediately told it would not happen. By this time, my PhD mentor told me it was time to expand my skill set and take on more responsibilities. After searching, I applied for, interviewed, and received the position of Director of Diversity and Inclusion at a newly established medical school. The learning curve was steep, but I took in everything medical education and its politics taught me. I stayed in that role for a decade.

The Unseen Burden as a Student Affairs Professional

As women of color and student affairs professionals, we are at times considered as the "other mothers" or "the ones that keep the machine running." Student affairs professionals historically served as the caretakers, *in loco* parentis, for the student body. For example, we will secure resources for a student to pay their tuition or seek out additional support in the form of tutoring. We look for those key indicators of student success to ensure that they are progressing in their development from a teen to young adult. While the trajectory has shifted to be more inclusive of students' rights for due process (Lee, 2011), just as a parent is with their child, we are often uncompensated in the emotional labor of supporting students, with the students being served and successful being seen as the compensation in and of itself. Emotional labor is not relegated to higher education, but is often silently attached to job descriptions, particularly when the role is one of caregiver or support staff and requires positive interactions (Guy & Newman, 2004). Through formal and informal means, employees learn how to control and display their emotions in a manner that aligns with the expectations of their job (Humphrey, 2022). When connected to race and unconscious bias, significant areas of training and development in our diversity, equity and inclusion positions, we hold the dual burden of being emotionally intelligent and holding space for others while suppressing our own emotions. Despite what shows up in our personal lives, the struggle to remain objective in the face of a dilemma is compounded when we serve as the safe space for others, but not having the chance to process for ourselves The COVID-19 is one example many can relate to as we navigated, supported, suppressed our own personal traumas and responded to the crisis in support of the institution and our students.

Caryn. A year and a half later after my daughter was born, my biological father passed, and divorced, I was at my emotional limit. Between the grief and postpartum sadness, I found myself working hard not to show any cracks in my professional demeanor. Additionally, I was put in an uncompromising position to release an employee due to inappropriate social media engagement with students arguing the tumultuous political events during that time period. Up until this point in my career, I didn't feel like it would be acceptable to show emotions other than happy, understanding or contentment because I was supposed to comfort other people, not be comforted. There was no space for my own emotions to show up in real time, even though life was happening in real time. The unbearable heaviness and hurt weighed on me trying to repair a carefully built bridge between students and administration. As much as I needed to have the uncomfortable conversations, because of the severity of the situation, and advice of human resources, I didn't. It would have put my own career in jeopardy at a particularly tenuous point in time. Every day after that moment felt like walking a tightrope with no net or no end in sight.

My immediate supervisor was helpful, allowing me to adjust my post-maternity leave schedule when needed, but everything seemed to be happening at the same time. The need to work harder to prove my dedication if I wasn't a mother loomed large. On the flip side, the expectation when I came home from work was that the student affairs professional would be left behind and the doting mother would take over. When married, I would ask for assistance and often was rebuffed, being told that whatever help I asked for would be taken care of at a later time. I took on a lot alone. Once we separated, I had to get strategic on where my help would come from, be it a sitter I paid for, someone to clean the house every couple of weeks, or his mother lending a hand. Between #BlackLivesMatter, recurring violence and protests, #OscarsSoWhite, not feeling like enough of a parent due to the divorce and split custody, keeping pace with a heavy workload, and the emotional labor of supporting students eventually I had a mental breakdown. I was beyond embarrassed and worse, what were the people at work going to think of me being out of the office? Would they even believe I needed a break, support, relief, additional help? After that, unsurprisingly, I was formally diagnosed with high functioning depression and anxiety. Days and weeks seemed to run together, I was running empty. Then the quickly spreading COVID-19 pandemic canceled everything. The early months of the pandemic opened up the opportunity to reflect on my role, the toll on my personal life, and the challenges to achievement. The stay-at-home order gave me permission to listen to my body and emotional health, putting them first without repercussion and fear of retribution. For the first time in my career, I could de-stress and not feel guilt for stepping away. It was also a heavy reminder that I could have done this all along, that the biggest skills missing from my toolbox were setting boundaries and asking for what I needed to be successful. The realization led me to make the vow to give myself whatever it is I need and not be apologetic for it.

Michelle. The unexpected burden and stress accompanied me as a graduate and professional student affairs staff. I faced many negative experiences in my adulthood that changed me as a person. First, in my first marriage I fell victim to domestic violence. Second, it was during my first-year as a doctoral student that I experienced misogyny and blatant disrespect. While these experiences caused me to have my own share of mental health challenges, questioning my every move, I turned to my profession to drown out my issues. I worked twice as hard seeking to prove and justify my belonging in the profession. Despite my own path to rebuild and heal, I never let it impact the needs of my students. Third, I faced reverse ageism from my colleagues and supervisors with my age being called into question based on the breadth of experiences and positions I was able to secure. Also, being labeled as "student" in many conversations, meetings or being called "young lady" in a room full of men when I carried the title as Director and was brought in to consult with to problem solve. The lack of respect burdened me, caused me to work from the state of underdog and employ my defense mechanisms.

The emotional labor of supporting students often led me to disinvest in myself and pour my life into the students. I have worked both in rural and urban communities serving diverse students. I remember when I worked as the Director and encouraging students to study abroad often meant I had to see them board the plane literally. The burden to make sure they secured their passports, for example,there was a student whose parent had a missing parent's name on his birth certificate which resulted in making a trip to the state records office because he could not secure his birth certificate locally. Or transporting an only child student to the airport because her mental and physically disabled mother could not and she had no other family to help that resulted in trying to stay up only to almost burn my house down from cooking and falling asleep. Another example of letting a homeless female student live with me until we were able to secure transitional housing for her or becoming the primary contact for a ward of state because she had no other family.

My burdens were with my students. While I thrived in my roles supporting students and fighting the injustices, my burdens became my students. It meant proving my worth by showing up and working countless hours, volunteering to be engaged and burning the midnight oil as a graduate student myself. Over the years, I have learned to take a stand for my own mental health. It was important to find my voice, advocate for myself and set boundaries. After going through my own therapy, and finding love again. I am proud to experience the myriad of success that came with becoming Dr. Mrs. Mom this time around. Although these transitions also impacted my career planning and priorities, and for many nights I grieved over the changes until I reimagined my next steps. Of course, the time off during COVID-19 helped and allowed me to build and sustain my family priorities. Drawing the conclusion, for the first time in my life, I don't have to do it all. Having a partner to do life, share responsibilities, I can focus my talents, skills and strategically align them to support the institution, colleagues, students while being true to self and my mental health. While I am not at the final stage in my career, I have learned that it is no longer a sprint but a journey.

THE CAUTIONARY TALE AS A
STUDENT AFFAIRS PROFESSIONAL

We are not the only ones that have expressed these dueling realities and multidimensional challenges that show up for us in our working lives. For many women who chose to be Dr. Mrs. Mom, the loss of economic ramifications in these roles have often clashed with social expectations. The purpose of our narrative was not to indicate a cookie-cutter pattern; rather it was a holistic journey of self-discovery and healing. Guided by our own lived experiences we have leaned on ourselves and others throughout our professional career. It is no longer about the institution; it is about integrating our authentic selves into our professional lives. And whether the cautionary tale is indeed cautionary at all, these are our stories to share to inspire and remind you that you are not alone.

ADVICE AND ENCOURAGING THOUGHTS TO THE
STUDENT AFFAIRS PROFESSIONAL

As potential student affairs practitioners entering the field, it is important to know that you are not alone. There's beauty in having a cadre of student affairs and DEI professionals to connect with when it feels like you're the only person dealing with complex situations that intersect with our lived experiences as partners, parents and professionals. We are all overcomers, and have navigated many life challenges, some we don't realize until we are older that such realities could have taken us down many dark places. Yet, we continue to show up for our students and the institution in which we work. As much as you pour into students, be sure others are pouring into you. Whether that is through a mentor, colleague you can share ideas and experiences or your own mental health professionals.

Inspired by motivational quotes, the practice of journaling, and networking, we find refuge in these outlets as systems of support to be and remain in student affairs. Know your worth and don't hesitate to challenge yourself to broaden or deepen your competencies in the profession. Embrace the subject matter of the student affairs profession and be willing to improve your skill set. Also recognize that it is okay to move on if you have hit a ceiling in your subject matter or institution. Don't be afraid to vocalize the systems of inequality, call it out for what it is, but don't be anyone's martyr or used as tokenism for the institution. Finally, affirm yourself regularly with affirmations such as "what is for me is for me, I will prepare for the opportunities, greater is coming." These motivational quotes along with spirituality center our thoughts and confidence to find balance in our personal and professional lives. We hope that throughout this chapter you were able to identify a few life lessons and things to do to turn lemons into lemonade, pivot when life challenges you and integrate balance to one's own journey.

REFERENCES

Collins, P. H. (2000). *Black feminist thought: Knowledge, consciousness, and the politics of empowerment*. Routledge.

Duggan, M. H. (2008). Noninstructional staff perceptions of the college climate. *New Directions for Community Colleges, 142*, 47–56.

Eisenmann, L. (2007, June). The impact of historical expectations on women's higher education. In *Forum on Public Policy Online: A Journal of the Oxford Round Table, Forum on Public Policy*.

Guy, M. E., & Newman, M. A. (2004). Women's jobs, men's jobs: Sex segregation and emotional labor. *Public Administration Review, 64*(3), 289–298.

Henderson, R. (2006). Time for a sea change. In S. Tregeagle (Ed.), *Balance: Real-life strategies for work/life balance*. Sea Change.

Humphrey, N. M. (2022). Racialized emotional labor: An unseen burden in the public sector. *Administration & Society, 54*(4), 741–758. https://doi.org/10.1177/00953997211037583

Jones, S. J., & Taylor, C. M. (2013). Work and life balance support of female midlevel noninstructional staff at community colleges. *Community College Journal of Research and Practice, 37*(12), 936–953.

Lee, P. (2011). The curious life of in loco parentis at American Universities. *Higher Education in Review, 8*, 65–90.

CHAPTER 11

BLACK IN WHITE SPACES

Ebony S. Cole

ABSTRACT

Being an educated Black professional in spaces dominated by Whites can be challenging. Black professionals are systematically subjected to racial and gendered bias fueled by the ideas of White superiority, delivered in the form of microaggressions. Compared to Black men, Black women encounter more cases of racial and gendered biases within the same setting. For example, when Black women challenge the policies and practices used to oppress them, they are often met with stereotypes and stigmas despite their character, education level, and professional experience. The false narrative that Black women are loud, unapproachable, and challenging to work with is deeply rooted in the dogma of the *angry Black woman*. In truth, Black women are no longer afraid to call out the negative antics used against us within society and the workplace.

BACKGROUND

Throughout my career, I have held mid-to-senior level administrator roles for predominantly White private, proprietary, and state institutions, where Whites make up 50% or more of their student population. My journey into higher education started when I worked as a cosmetology instructor for a local beauty school in my home state. I watched as many of my students struggled with the day-to-day aspects of trying to escape the perpetual cycle of living in poverty. I'll never forget the overwhelming joy I felt once my students went up for and passed their state boards and later found success

Still Working While Black:
The Untold Stories of Student Affairs Practitioners, pp. 105–115
Copyright © 2023 by Information Age Publishing
www.infoagepub.com
All rights of reproduction in any form reserved.

within the beauty industry. During this time, I developed a passion for helping other individuals during their educational journeys.

One Word That Describes My Higher Education Experience

As a result of being doubly marginalized (i.e., being Black and female), the best word to describe my experience working in higher education is *resilient*. According to Moya and Goenechea (2022), resilience is an opportunity to learn and grow when faced with adversities. Because Black women are significantly disadvantaged and often psychologically and occupationally victimized by persons with privileged identities (Kim & O'Brien, 2018) within the workplace, our emotional fortitude, independence, and self-sacrifice are the mitigating factors driving our ability to persevere (Jones et al., 2021). In addition, our self-efficacy (i.e., the belief in oneself to achieve goals and complete tasks) level grounds our coping abilities when challenged in the workplace (Jordan, 2020). We are resilient because despite our circumstances we still show up every day for the students we serve.

The Negative Effects of Being Black in White Spaces

As a Black woman in higher education, my challenges concerning my race and gender are linked to my personal experiences involving microaggressions and discrimination and my inability to advance into a senior-level position within predominantly White spaces. Within these spaces lies a system that excludes, ignores, and oppresses Black women (Shahid et al., 2018). This system comprises racial and gendered prejudice, bias, and inequitable approaches, which have created hostile working environments (Clarke, 2018). Nair and Vollhardt (2020) added that the racial and gendered identities of Black women intersect with their advantages and disadvantages within the workplace. Howe and Rockhill (2020) added that Black women often must contend with how the dominant White culture views their identity, including sexism, within these environments. According to Glasener et al. (2019), which could lead to a downward spiral for Black women who mentally struggle while navigating the complexities of an environment dominated by Whites.

I'll never forget the time when I accepted a position at a small liberal arts college. I was super excited about the prospect of assisting students as they strive to overcome financial barriers that would otherwise prevent them from obtaining a college degree. Yet, it never went unnoticed that I was the only Black person in my department. During the first week of my employment, I received an email from another Black administrator who summoned me for a meeting. Being new to the institution, I was somewhat nervous about meeting an upper-level administrator, but I saw a Black man standing before me when I got to his office, and I was immediately at ease. We started conversing about where I had come from and what led me to the institution. He then shared with me that he would quietly get the word out that another "sista"[sic] had come on board, and I was quickly introduced to the rest of the community of Black administrators across campus. And because this was early in my career, I was ecstatic about the opportunity to expand my professional network. Yet, it never crossed my mind that the vast majority of my future encounters with these individuals would be geared toward discussions surrounding the mistreatment, microaggressions, bias, and acts of racial discrimination that I would later experience at that institution.

This network of support from my Black colleagues felt more like a secret society since little attention was given to the experiences of Blacks working in predominantly White spaces, which supports the notion that within these institutions, Blacks are viewed merely as tokens (Clarke, 2018; Cooke & Sánchez, 2019). Adserias et al. (2017) state that predominantly White institutions (PWI) have a history of viewing diversity as strategic importance for their agendas rather than an encompassing effort to change the workplace culture.

For example, Scott (2016) identified four considerable advantages of employing Blacks within a PWI:

1. The perception is that discrimination is no longer a hindrance to career opportunities;
2. Increased representation of Blacks employed;
3. Positive achievements for student academic success;
4. More role models of color on campus.

Scott's claim resonates with me as I have never worked for an institution where I was not the only Black administrator in my respective department. In fact, I've always felt like I was a diversity hire, which to me supports Scott's perspective that these PWI will hire a limited number of Black professionals, specifically in a mid-to-senior level role, simply to give off the impression that discrimination is no longer a hindrance to our career opportunities. However, the truth is that our racial and gendered identities are always considered by our White counterparts when opportunities for advancement are present. A great example of how race and gender are regarded for senior-level roles is when I shared with one of my White colleagues how I aspire to become a college president someday. He responded by saying he could see me being a president of a Historically Black College or University (HBCU) instead of a PWI because I don't fit the image of a president within a PWI. When he said this to me, I abruptly ended the conversation and went on about my business. I ended the conversation because his statement was a reminder of the racial bias that most Whites consciously and subconsciously have toward Blacks, especially us Black women.

As I drove home later that day, I can recall the conversation that had previously taken place between this White man and me, and the more I thought about it, the more I felt a rush of anger. I was pissed, to say the least, because who was he to tell me that I would never become president of a PWI and that I would only be a good fit at an HBCU. As I continued my drive home, I thought about Kimberle Crenshaw's teaching on intersectionality. In the late 1980s and early 1990s, Crenshaw (1989) coined the term intersectionality to highlight how one's identity (i.e., Black and women; Black and male;) can intersect with the multiple layers of oppression Blacks and other marginalized groups face in America (Haynes et al., 2020; Moorosi et al., 2018).

Here I am, a young educated Black woman being told by an older White man that there's a restriction concerning my aspirations of becoming a college president one day solely based on my race and gender. Never mind the fact that I possess a doctorate in education with a specialization in higher education leadership coupled with a Master of Business Administration. I mean, I know that I am more than capable of leading a predominantly White institution in addition to an HBCU someday.

You see, due to my race and gender, I know that I have to work twice as hard to be successful compared to my White counterparts in the workplace. Therefore, I am always mindful to ensure that my work integrity remains intact. For example, I would complete tasks quicker and more accurately than my colleagues, and, as a result, I was required to take on their workload due to their delayed productivity. When this would occur, my White colleagues would call me a *show-off*, which would irritate me a lot because I was far from that. By calling me a show-off, it was as if they felt I thought I was better than them due to my high work performance and work ethic. When the truth is, I knew I had to always be on top of my game since I was held more accountable for any mistakes or mishaps I made. Therefore, I took pride in my work and my ability to finish things on time, and because of my work ethic, other department heads would call on me to partake in special projects and be part of special committees. However, while I was honored to be called upon, many of my White counterparts were not too thrilled—especially my former director, who was a White woman. I can recall her telling me that she gets paid the big bucks to think and that other department heads should be reaching out to her first.

As the toxicity within my work environment continued to increase, I began to experience bouts of anxiety due to the recurring microaggressions I was encountering from my White counterparts. Williams et al. (2020)

defined racial microaggression as subtle, daily, intentional, and unintentional racial slights committed against members of a racialized group. Also, Baalbaki (2019) found that microaggressions adversely affect Black women's mental and physical well-being (Robinson-Wood et al., 2015). I needed an outlet fast.

I would frequently meet with other Black professionals on campus and share my negative experiences as they would occur. I thought I was strong enough to handle acts of discrimination and microaggressions once they happened to me, but the truth is that I was not as strong as I thought. I often sat in my car and cried during my lunch break because I felt like no one was listening. On several occasions, I reached out to the vice president of enrollment management to request a meeting to address the racial disparities and toxicity I was experiencing. But to no avail, my requests were ignored. And by this point, the reoccurring acts of microaggressions and racial discrimination within my department started to take a toll on me mentally and physically, and I began to question my purpose.

According to Galupo and Resnick (2016), microaggressions consist of microassults, microinsults, and microinvalidations. Each form of microaggressions has a unique characteristic that highlights the intentional and unintentional acts of discrimination against Blacks. Turaga (2020) recognized microinsults as the involuntary act that conveys rudeness and insensitivity towards individuals to demean their racial heritage. Turaga later described microassaults as conscious and intentional discrimination and microinvalidations as verbal comments to exclude, negate, or nullify others' thoughts, feelings, and experiences. And Simatele (2018) added that when microaggressions remain invisible, individuals begin to think that racism no longer exists or that the incident is isolated and caused by the victim. And because I was one of very few Blacks to speak up against how the microaggressions displayed by my White counterparts were affecting me, I was often thought to be the sole cause for issues surrounding my race within my department. In reality, I know that my negative experience was shaped by the shared attitudes and beliefs geared towards the idea of White superiority and White dominance within this institution.

Similarly, like microaggressions, endemic racism has become so pervasive and ever-present that it is unrecognizable or invisible to most individuals (Baciu, 2020; Ogbonnaya-Ogburu et al., 2020). Baciu (2020) describes endemic racism as normalized discrimination within a given society. Despite the historical events surrounding racism that negatively affected Blacks in this country, racism continues to impact the community as it influences and guides today's economic and political constructs (Shain, 2020). According to Moore (2019), when the status quo of racism is maintained, it propels Whites' interest and advancements in a given society (Howe & Rockhill, 2020). We see the extent of Moore's perspective in predominantly

White institutions through the limited number of Black professionals in senior-level positions since most senior-level roles are acquired through the *good old boy* network, which is comprised of White men. As a result of this network of White men, Black professionals are not advancing into senior-most and executive-level leadership roles within these PWI at the same rate as Whites. And the few Blacks in senior-level positions within the same setting often have more negative experiences brought forth by their racial and gendered identities than any other racial group in the same place.

For example, I can vividly recall where my race brought forth challenges within the workplace when I served as a senior-level administrator to a small staff of all White women. Within the first couple of weeks of being on the job, I was met with resistance from my subordinates. These women would challenge my intellect and undermine my leadership ability by using the stereotypical idea that I was an angry Black woman. For example, I would hold weekly staff meetings and communicate via email when appropriate because I believe in transparency. Yet, it was brought to my attention that my entire team contacted our human resource department to complain about the tone of my emails. It was no secret that these women were using their privileged identities to make my time with the institution hell with the hopes of me resigning from my position. However, little did they know that I was very cognizant of my environment and their intent. And unbeknown to my staff, I voiced my concerns early on about their resistance to the vice president of enrollment management and human resource. Though my concerns were heard, I was not supported by upper management, including the institution's human resource department. This lack of support made me realize that my Blackness was not welcomed on that campus.

Because of my experience, I gained a new level of understanding concerning the term glass ceiling. In the 1980s, Ann Morrison coined the term glass ceiling to highlight professional women's invisible barriers while striving to achieve advanced roles (Saleem et al., 2017). According to Beckwith et al. (2016), the paradigm presented by the glass ceiling is especially problematic for the doubly marginalized women who experience problems and challenges in preparation for careers and advancement within higher education. Because of my lack of support from upper management and my staff at this PWI. I immediately begin applying for employment back in my home state. And for months, as I waited for a response from one of the positions I had applied for, I started to isolate myself at work. I would show up to work daily with the sole purpose of doing my job and my job only, as I began to care less about the many issues outside of the scope of my responsibilities that were going on around me at that time. Once I got the call to interview for a position back in my home state, I was relieved, and once an offer was made, I gladly accepted the job.

Opportunities That My Race and Gender Have Brought to My Professional Experiences

As a higher education professional, my race has afforded me the opportunity to serve on committees geared toward improving diversity, equity, and inclusion across the campus. Equally important, I can support Black and minority students differently from my White colleagues, as I understand the difficulties many students face while attending college. As a first-generation college student, I know the complexities of living in poverty and what it feels like not to have a great deal of support from family. According to Wilfong and Cirino (2021), the effects of poverty are not limited to the socio-economic and health-related challenges that impoverished individuals face, as deprivation is also linked to the inequalities that affect them. Therefore, the opportunities that my race and gender bring in higher education are related to my ability to bring forth a different perspective and a sense of clarity during the decision-making process that impacts Black students from low socioeconomic communities.

Tips/Strategies on How to Successfully Navigate the Challenges of Working in White Spaces

Be your authentic self—As Black professionals, we often try to make meaning of our experiences through our professional identities and associations (Wilson et al., 2016). For example, in many cases, we will code-switch as a strategic and conscious effort not to display our racial and cultural identities (Bush, 2020). However, because code-switching is parallel to imposter syndrome, Black professionals feel like they live a double life in these environments due to altering their image, personalities, and demeanor while in White-dominated spaces (Collins et al., 2020; Edwards, 2019).

Therefore, it is imperative to remain true to yourself by holding onto your morals and values. This facet is linked to what Erving Goffman describes as impression management. According to Goffman (1959), individuals have strong motives for controlling the impression they give and receive while in the presence of others. Impression management is essential for Blacks working in predominantly White spaces because your intellect and professionalism may be challenged by White counterparts and sometimes by students. Therefore, you are highly encouraged to be comfortable with who you are as a Black professional and know that you are just as qualified as your White counterparts despite their perception of you.

Find Support—I strongly recommend establishing a network of support. This web of support can consist of a religious leader, professional therapist, support group, mentor, or an individual you trust that can genuinely help guide you through tough times. Rasheem et al. (2018) found that

Black mentors provide the best emotional support, guidance, confidence, and empowerment to other Black professionals struggling with workplace inequalities. Conversely, Pope and Edwards (2016) found that Black women benefit from developing professional relationships with other Black women who also grapple with the intersectional inequalities of being both Black and a woman within predominately White institutions.

Affirmation for Inspiration

"Your name is being mentioned in rooms your feet haven't entered yet. God is going to do something amazing in your life; keep moving forward" (Anonymous, n.d.). This affirmation is in a frame in my office. Each day when I arrive to work, it is the first thing I see as it is a reminder of my infectious character, professionalism, and work ethic. In addition, this affirmation has significantly impacted my life, as several students, parents, and colleagues (past, present, and future) have known of me despite ever meeting them. Therefore, I believe faith without work is dead, and my faith keeps me grounded in the affirmation.

Final Thoughts

While being a Black woman in higher education has its challenges, I need the world to know that I am an educated Black woman who's not afraid to call out the racial antics used against me within society and the workplace. I want the world to know that my purpose in working in higher education is to be a voice for marginalized students and to guide and support them along their journeys. Despite all the adversities, I may go through because I am a strong advocate for education, I believe education is the pathway to overcoming poverty.

REFERENCES

Adserias, R. P., Charleston, L. J., & Jackson, J. F. (2017). What style of leadership is best suited to direct organizational change to fuel institutional diversity in higher education? *Race Ethnicity and Education, 20*(3), 315–331. https://doi.org/10.1080/13613324.2016.1260233

Baalbaki, M. (2019). Gendered racism, psychological distress, and the strong Black woman. *Journal of Clinical and Translational Science, 3*, 107. http://doi.org/10.1017/cts.2019.244

Baciu, L. (2020). Reading beyond the label: Implications of the critical race theory for the social work practice with Roma people. *Social Work Review/Revista de Asistenta Sociala, 3*, 79–98.

Beckwith, A. L., Carter, D. R., & Peters, T. (2016). The underrepresentation of African American women in executive leadership: What's getting in the way? *Journal of Business Studies Quarterly, 7*(4), 115–134.

Bush, A. A. (2020). A conceptual framework for exploring the experiences of underrepresented racial minorities in pharmacy school. *American Journal of Pharmaceutical Education, 84*(1), 37–46. https://doi.org/10.5688/ajpe7544

Clarke, J. A. (2018). Explicit bias. *Northwestern University Law Review, 113*(3), 505–586.

Collins, K. H., Price, E. F., Hanson, L., & Neaves, D. (2020). Consequences of stereotype threat and imposter syndrome: The personal journey from STEM-practitioner to STEM-educator for four women of color. *The Journal of Culture & Education, 19*(4), 161–180.

Cooke, N. A., & Sánchez, J. O. (2019). Getting it on the record: Faculty of color in library and information science. *Journal of Education for Library and Information Science, 60*(3), 169–181. https://doi.org/10.3138/jelis.60.3.01

Crenshaw, K. (1989). Demarginalizing the intersection of race and sex: A Black feminist critique of antidiscrimination doctrine, feminist theory and antiracist politics. *University of Chicago Legal Forum*, 139–168.

Edwards, C. W. (2019). Overcoming imposter syndrome and stereotype threat: Reconceptualizing the definition of a scholar. *The Journal of Culture and Education, 18*(1), 3.

Galupo, M. P., & Resnick, C. A. (2016). Experiences of LGBT microaggressions in the workplace: Implications for policy. In T Köllen (Ed.), *Sexual orientation and transgender issues in organizations* (pp. 271–287). https://doi.org/10.1007/978-3-319-29623-4_16

Glasener, K. M., Martell, C. A., & Posselt, J. R. (2019). Framing diversity: Examining the place of race in institutional policy and practice post-affirmative action. *Journal of Diversity in Higher Education, 12*(1), 3–16. https://doi.org/10.1037/dhe0000086

Goffman, E. (1959). *The presentation of self in everyday life*. Anchor Books.

Haynes, C., Taylor, L., Mobley, S. D., Jr., & Haywood, J. (2020). Existing and resisting: The pedagogical realities of Black, critical men and women faculty. *The Journal of Higher Education, 91*(5), 698–721.

Howe, J. E., & Rockhill, C. A. (2020). "Feelings That Others Won't Necessarily Have": Experiences of Black athletic administrators navigating the collegiate athletic setting. *Journal of Issues in Intercollegiate Athletics*, 170–188.

Jones, M. K., Harris, K. J., & Reynolds, A. A. (2021). In their own words: The meaning of the strong black woman schema among black U.S. college women. *Sex Roles, 84*(5–6), 347–359. https://doi.org/10.1007/s11199-020-01170-w

Jordan, C. R. (2020). *Self-efficacy and mentorship on women of color in academic administrative leadership roles: A quantitative comparative cross-sectional study* (Publication No. 28154379) [Doctoral dissertations, Northcentral University]. ProQuest Dissertations and Thesis Global.

Kim, Y. H., & O'Brien, K. M. (2018). Assessing women's career barriers across racial/ethnic groups: The perception of barriers scale. *Journal of Counseling Psychology, 65*(2), 226–238. https://doi.org/10.1037/cou0000251

Moore, R. (2019). Whiteness=politeness: interest-convergence in Australian history textbooks, 1950–2010. *Critical Discourse Studies, 17*(1), 111. https://doi.org/10.1080/17405904.2019.1637760

Moorosi, P., Fuller, K., & Reilly, E. (2018). Leadership and intersectionality: Constructions of successful leadership among Black women school principals in three different contexts. *Management in Education, 32*(4), 152-159. https://doi.org/10.1177/0892020618791006

Moya, J., & Goenechea, M. (2022). An approach to the unified conceptualization, definition, and characterization of social resilience. *International Journal of Environmental Research and Public Health, 19*(9), 5746. https://doi.org/10.3390/ijerph19095746

Nair, R., & Vollhardt, J. R. (2020). Intersectionality and relations between oppressed groups: Intergroup implications of beliefs about intersectional differences and commonalities. *Journal of Social Issues, 76*(4), 993–1013. https://doi.org/10.1111/josi.12409

Ogbonnaya-Ogburu, I. F., Smith, A. D., To, A., & Toyama, K. (2020). Critical race theory for HCI. *In proceedings of the 2020 CHI conference on human factors in computing systems,* 1–16. http://doi.org/10.1145/3313831.3376392

Pope, E. C., & Edwards, K. T. (2016). Curriculum home placing as complicated conversation: (re)narrating the mentoring of Black women doctoral students. *Gender & Education, 28*(6), 769–785. https://doi.org/10.1080/09540253.2016.1221898

Rasheem, S., Alleman, A. S., Mushonga, D., Anderson, D., & Ofahengaue Vakalahi, H. F. (2018). Mentor-shape: Exploring the mentoring relationships of Black women in doctoral programs. *Mentoring & Tutoring: Partnership in Learning, 26*(1), 50–69. https://doi.org/10.1080/13611267.2018.1445443

Robinson-Wood, T., Balogun-Mwangi, O., Fernandes, C., Popat-Jain, A., Boadi, N., Matsumoto, A., & Zhang, X. (2015). Worse than blatant racism: A phenomenological investigation of microaggressions among Black women. *Journal of Ethnographic & Qualitative Research, 9*(3), 221–236.

Saleem, S., Rafiq, A., & Yusaf, S. (2017). Investigating the glass ceiling phenomenon: An empirical study of glass ceiling's effects on selection-promotion and female effectiveness. *South Asian Journal of Business Studies, 6*(3), 297–313. https://doi.org/10.1108/SAJBS-04-2016-0028

Scott, D. (2016). Recruiting and retaining African American male administrators at predominantly white institutions. *Urban Education Research & Policy Annuals, 4*(1). https://scholar.google.com/

Shahid, N. N., Nelson, T., & Cardemil, E. V. (2018). Lift every voice: Exploring the stressors and coping mechanisms of Black college women attending predominantly White institutions. *Journal of Black Psychology, 44*(1), 3–24. https://doi.org/10.1177/0095798417732415

Shain, F. (2020). Race matters: confronting the legacy of empire and colonialism. *British Journal of Sociology of Education, 41*(2), 272–280. https://doi.org/10.1080/01425692.2020.1717104

Simatele, M. (2018). A cross-cultural experience of microaggression in academia: A personal reflection. *Education as Change, 22*(3), 1–23. https://upjournals.co.za/index.php/EAC/article/view/3132

Turaga, R. (2020). Managing microaggressions at work. *IUP Journal of Soft Skills,* *14*(3), 42–51.

Wilfong, J., & Cirino, A. (2021). How social workers can address poverty in America. *Reflections: Narratives of Professional Helping, 27*(2), 71–77.

Williams, Q., Williams, B. M., & Brown, L. C. (2020). Exploring Black girl magic: Identity development of Black first-gen college women. *Journal of Diversity in Higher Education.* https://doi-org/10.1037/dhe0000294

Wilson, M. E., Liddell, D. L., Hirschy, A. S., & Pasquesi, K. (2016). Professional identity, career commitment, and career entrenchment of midlevel student affairs professionals. *Journal of College Student Development, 57*(5), 557–572. https://doi.org /10.1353/csd.2016.0059

CHAPTER 12

I AM A MENTOR, LIKE IT OR NOT!

Andrew Johnson

ABSTRACT

Working in student affairs, or the trenches as I call it, because you are on the ground, in an ever-changing day-to-day environment working with students. You are constantly engaging with students, both formally and informally, in a variety of situations, many of which are unpredictable. These interactions often lead to a mentoring relationship, whether you like it or not. As a Black student affairs professional, you are a mentor and will be called upon to mentor students of color, especially if you work at a predominantly White institution. Tareef (2013) describes mentoring as a process in which an experienced person guides the mentee through developing their own ideas that will contribute to their learning and personal and professional competence.

Due to the nature of your role on your campus and being Black, students of color will naturally gravitate towards you as they seek to develop a sense of belonging on campus. Black students are often afraid of intimidated by faculty and upper-level administration, but your role will often be more casual and approachable. It is easier for them to engage with us because we are often the most visible folks on campus working in places where they can be more relaxed.

The question or challenge is how you manage the pressure of providing this much-needed mentoring to young Black students while navigating your personal and professional needs as a Black student affairs professional.

Still Working While Black:
The Untold Stories of Student Affairs Practitioners, pp. 117–123
Copyright © 2023 by Information Age Publishing
www.infoagepub.com

I AM A MENTOR, LIKE IT OR NOT!

My Path to a Career in Student Affairs

Like many others I have met working in this field, my professional path took an unexpected turn into student affairs which has spanned almost 19 years. My undergraduate degree is in sports administration, and I intended to work in the sports industry. Not in a million years did I think I would work in higher education, let alone student affairs. In 2003 a year removed receiving my undergraduate degree from Lock Haven University of Pennsylvania, I was fortunate to gain full-time employment as a health and physical education teacher and coach at a K–12 private school in my hometown of Philadelphia, which was also not part of my plan. In the fall of that same year, I accepted my first role as a part-time Division III women's basketball assistant coach in higher education and student affairs. Of course, at this time, I had no master plan of continuing towards a career in student affairs; I was coaching basketball. However, I began fully immersing myself in the campus community to best support my student-athletes. As a young professional, I was already beginning to mentor students, albeit they were very close to my age! I am still connected to many of these young women almost 20 years later.

Those interactions and experiences as a young assistant basketball coach led me to pursue a career as a community college athletic director, where I developed both my leadership skills and my desire to serve students. As an athletic director, I honed my mentoring skills while working with student-athletes and other students on campus while fully immersing myself in the campus community. Hence, I was able to work with a variety of student groups. I also began to mentor staff adding a new piece to the puzzle. My coaches were part-time and mostly new coaches looking to get started in the business, so they sought a lot of guidance from me about the profession and even sought advice about their personal lives.

I held two athletic director positions at two different institutions for eleven years until COVID-19 halted athletics in the Northeastern United States. And it was during this time that I developed a sense of what student affairs is and what being a student affairs professional truly means. So here is where I committed to serving students!

The crossroads brought on by COVID-19 came at a perfect time for me as I was completing my doctoral studies at the University of Pittsburgh and seeking a new career within higher education. I was fortunate that my institution placed me in a new role during this time. First, I could remain employed, but it also allowed me to experience another "side of the house," which was serving in a director role in the enrollment management department, which gave me a new perspective and allowed me to work with folks outside of student support. This temporary role was followed by my transition into my desired field of diversity, equity, and inclusion. I served as an assistant director of diversity, inclusion and belonging at a small liberal arts college. I was grateful for that position as I took on a lot of leadership roles while learning the ropes of a new field. Again, I could get fully immersed in this role by supporting other departments due to staff shortages, which allowed me to gain more valuable skills as a professional. I was willing to do anything in this position because I knew ultimately, it would lead to my desired position as a director of multicultural student affairs at a larger institution.

Are you wondering how I went from athletic director to DEI work? My interest in pursuing a position in Diversity, Equity, and Inclusion came from that natural desire to mentor students of color throughout their college degree process. That desire to support the students I was working with at the community college level steered me to lead diversity, equity, and inclusion initiatives on a volunteer basis. I saw firsthand the impact and the importance of Diversity, Equity, and Inclusion work, which has motivated me to continue working in the field of student affairs, mainly focused on DEI work.

The One Word to Describe My Experience as Student Affairs Professional

Those who work in student affairs at any time will understand what I am about to say. Working in student affairs is an amazing but sometimes exhausting experience at the same time, and several words or characteristics come to mind when attempting to describe what it is that we do. The one word that comes to my mind to explain what it is like for me is FLEXIBLE! Merriam-Webster (n.d.) defines flexibility as being characterized by a ready capability to adapt to new, different, or changing requirements. Every day is new! Every day is different! Every day the requirements change! No one year, semester, month, week, day, or even hour is the same. Understanding this concept helps you embrace what may seem like chaos at times. When institutions restructure, adopt new goals or strategic plans, a crisis occurs on campus, or perhaps a pandemic happens, the folks in student affairs are always prepared to handle these situations, often without hesitation. That is what day-to-day life is like in student affairs; we put out fires!

These new and different days make working in student affairs both an amazing and exhausting experience. The days often seem chaotic, but they present opportunities to authentically work with and connect with students. The same goes for the relationships you develop with colleagues. It is here in the trenches where mentoring connections and relationships are cultivated.

CHALLENGES THAT I HAVE FACED AS A STUDENT AFFAIRS PROFESSIONAL

Many thoughts ran through my mind when I reflected on some of the challenges my race has had on my professional experience. I've experienced and witnessed macroaggressions, microaggressions, and outright racism towards students a few times, so those are always tricky situations to navigate, particularly when trying to advise a student or peer who is unable to manage the situation themselves.

The one challenge that has had the most significant impact on my career is not being taken seriously. It was this challenge; specifically, that was one of the reasons I decided to pursue my doctorate. I wanted to gain the proverbial "seat at the table" I wanted the work I was doing to be taken seriously, which was mostly outside my job description as an athletic director. I often felt like a foot soldier, put on the ground to do the dirty work, but I wanted to be a leader and impact change. Being Black and an athletic director, I felt as if I was being put in an extra-large box of only knowing about and being able to facilitate athletics but I knew I was capable of impacting change at my institution. Black males are often stereotyped as only being able to contribute in the areas of sports and entertainment. It took some time but continuing to push the envelope and engage in spaces where I may not have always been wanted allowed me to gain a bit more credibility; however, I was still not able to infiltrate the spaces that would affect the policies and procedures and make significant change.

The burnout you've heard about is real! Student affairs professionals face burnout, which can be magnified for Black folks in this field. As institutions are now focusing on recruiting, retaining, and graduating students of color at higher rates, folks on campus will look at us to provide answers and insight and often place blame. The wild part is we do this to ourselves as well. We are heavily relied on to be mentors for students and staff. Not only are you responsible for the duties within your job description and working many hours, but you are also relied on to be the network and support for students and staff of color. We are already under pressure to perform because of a history of stereotypes but couple that with a lack of representation on campuses around the country, your skin color can put you in the position to become that mentor or advocate, whether you like it or not.

Opportunities That I Have Been Afforded as a Student Affairs Professional

As a student affairs professional, my race and gender are a gift and a curse. The curse is explained in the previous section; it leads to not being taken seriously at times and burnout. However, if kept in perspective and managed correctly, I have treasured the opportunities it provides me. First and foremost, with my history of working at Predominantly White Institutions, my being a Black male makes me more of an expert at times in leading the work that I do, which has given me an upper hand in getting involved at various levels of an institution.

In the previous section, I talked about not being taken seriously; it meant that sometimes I had to fight within my field of expertise to gain credibility. It also meant I had to fight extra hard to gain credibility in areas outside my interest. For me, I was one of few people of color leading an athletic department; therefore, needing to fight outside of the walls of my institution. Within my institution, I had to gain credibility outside of athletics and show that I could impact the institution's overall mission. Again, this is part of what led me to attend the University of Pittsburgh's EdD program. This is what drove my desire to do more!

I have faced burnout during my career, all due to the pressure to show my worth, my value, and that I could excel in my field. Mostly the burnout comes from the constant need to be available to mentor young students of color because I am most times the only professional of color they have to connect with on campus. Whether I liked it or not, I knew they were looking up to me; I also knew that new professionals were looking to me for guidance on navigating the system. My impact was evident in the words that were expressed toward me by students after their time working with me. I've also had staff members come to me for advice and express gratitude for something I said or did for them. You will inevitably be a mentor, and like I said, whether you like it or not.

Tips to Navigate a Career In Student Affairs

A career in student affairs can be gratifying, but just as you were likely told as an undergraduate student, it is what you make of it. Just as we preach to our students the importance of getting involved, we as professionals must do the same. Getting involved as a professional means seeking professional development opportunities and finding local, regional, and national conferences to attend. These conferences can be directly related to your field or indirectly associated with higher education; they all tie together. Attending virtual conferences is much easier now, but you will not get the same networking experiences as being in person. Most of what I've learned about programming, management, and being a professional comes from attending conferences. While at conferences, seek mentors; you may be surprised how much folks are willing to help you throughout your career. Furthermore, do not be afraid to contact someone via phone, email, or social media to connect.

Be willing to cross-train and learn other areas of higher education; this will increase your marketability and, more importantly, your ability to serve students. Folks in higher education tend to work within silos but getting to know how multiple areas function will only benefit you. Doing this may require you to volunteer and work outside your typical hours or duties, which we know is a challenge and leads to my next point.

As discussed earlier, burnout in higher education can be very real; you must maintain a work-life balance. The best way to do this is to set boundaries and openly communicate with staff and supervisors. You cannot give your best when you are not at your best mentally and physically. Therefore, take time off, engage in your family life, and disconnect from work email and phone calls during non-business hours! As an athletic director, a mentor once told me, "we watch other people's kids play games more than we watch our own." It took me some time to understand that, but after six or seven years, I finally understood he was talking about work-life balance.

My biggest tip, which I've sometimes learned the hard way throughout my career, is to ensure everything you do fits within the college's strategic plan and goals! I faced trouble at times building projects, being unable to gain buy in and support. I also had to answer to supervisors or senior administration when I didn't do this. Tying everything into one of these groups helps keep your work focused. It makes it easier to bring others on board for collaboration, and it will make it easier to answer any questions about why you are doing a particular initiative or project. Sticking to the institutional strategic plan and goals will also allow for appropriate data to be used for reporting purposes.

What Keeps Me Going!

At times it's going to feel like the institution is on fire, and all you are doing is trying to put it out. I like to think of that analogy as an excellent way to describe the behind-the-scenes in higher education, mostly student affairs. I focus on students as a student-centered professional in all that I do. Although I work for my boss, my institution, I serve my students! I tell myself daily as I drive to work or when I find myself in a meeting that could quickly go left! I also have a student-focused sign on my desk to remind me and those who enter my office what is important to me. So, when times or days get rough in the office, take a deep breath, and remember why you do the work.

CONCLUSION

My perspective comes from the lens of my personal experience. I am a first-generation student from a low-income, inner-city household. I didn't really understand what I was going through during my years as a student, and it showed in my performance. My aha moment didn't come until I began working in student affairs; I was able to put myself in the shoes of the students I was working with. That empathy came naturally to me and drove me to be sure they got better as students.

REFERENCES

Flexible. (n.d.). In *Merriam-Webster's online dictionary.* https://www.merriam-webster.com/dictionary/flexible

Tareef, A. B. (2013). The relationship between mentoring and career development of higher education faculty members. *College Student Journal, 47,* 703–710. https://www.projectinnovation.com/

CONCLUSION

Antione D. Tomlin and Carl Mackey

The stories and experiences shared echo a salient point about the narratives concerning Blackness. That point is the experience of blackness, although containing many common experiences, is not monolithic. Much like the contents of a mosaic, the experiences of Blackness are unique to each individual who both self-identifies, or is otherwise identified, as African American in these United States. Mosaics are comprised of materials of different shapes, sizes, and textures. Smooth stones can be juxtaposed with jagged glass, which may border porous terra cotta. And though the elements of a mosaic are so varied, their inclusion, arrangement, and intentionality are necessary to see the image they are meant to portray. This is why, as Black people, we must continue to add all of our individual and collective narratives to the backdrop of majority White America. This addition makes the image of our histories, struggles, and earned places in this country clearer. The narratives in this book help to add to the fullness of our collective narrative by allowing Black practitioners to stand in their truths and tell their stories. These stories not only come with caution but also with hope and advice. Each theme centered around the commonality found in the stories and offered words of wisdom to those on the path of student affairs, as well as those seeking to begin their journey. We hope these voices will add to the collective consciousness, building this mosaic that is an everlasting image and tribute to us as a people and bringing our story, ALL of our story, into focus. We note that the conclusion of this book is crafted to provide additional encouragement and support for Black student affairs practitioners.

Still Working While Black:
The Untold Stories of Student Affairs Practitioners, pp. 125–130
Copyright © 2023 by Information Age Publishing
www.infoagepub.com

THEME 1: I SAID WHAT I SAID: MY VOICE MATTERS!

This theme continues the irrevocable idea that Black women's voices are muted in higher education. As they are major players in the field, they contribute greatly to the body of knowledge for Student Affairs research. They are the backbone of support for Black students and other students of color in postsecondary education. These authors share their stories, frustrations, and suggestions in the hope of helping other Black women find, use, and protect their own voices. After all, a narrative cannot be heard without a voice.

Don't Do It on Your Own: Find Your Circle of Allies

Each of the authors under this theme espoused the need for support inside and outside of the institution for which you work. According to the authors, a mentor, a touchstone, a sounding board, or even a "Circle of Sisters" will provide the release, support, and guidance you will need to survive and thrive in student affairs. Black women need to find other Black women who move in the same spaces that they do so that the compassion and care coming from this sisterhood are built from shared knowledge and perspective of the experience of Black women in student affairs.

When You Come Through, Come Through: Be Your Authentic Self

The concept of representation flows through the assertions made by the authors that, to exist in the oppressive spaces of student affairs, it is paramount that you be yourself. Not just be who you are in terms of your personality, although that is part of the deal, representing yourself in all of your fullness and Blackness in these spaces is necessary. This authenticity of self is not only important for your own well-being, but it is another way to support Black students who are struggling in these spaces just like you. When they see someone like them daring to present their authentic selves in an environment that tells them to assimilate to succeed, they see an example of success walking in authenticity.

How Did You Get Here?: Remember Your Purpose

As a professional in student affairs, you can often get mired in the tarpit of being overworked, underpaid, underappreciated, and the day-to-day war raging on Black women in student affairs. Amid constant micro- and macroaggressions, the undermining of your voice and professionalism and the looming oppression can distract you from your purpose. The authors suggest that, when things seem insurmountable, remember your reason for choosing student affairs as a career: the students. It would be a safe bet to assume that most, if not all, Black student affairs professionals are in the field to serve students, particularly Black students, and other students of color. Connecting with this sense of service, dedication, and responsibility to students that is contained in your purpose for your profession will help you weather the storms that undoubtedly come.

THEME 2: AT THE END OF THE DAY, I GOT ME!

Working and living life as a Black student affairs professional can be brutal. Black women, in particular, have a tumultuous journey fraught with obstacles, oppression, and unrealistic expectations. It is a daily struggle to stay connected to your purpose and goals when you are perceived as, and consequently treated as, a threat or, even worse, a non-threat. Black professionals climbing the ladder of success in student affairs must gird themselves with tools and strategies to rebuke spirits of malintent and those who would derail their good intentions. Choosing a life of service is hard enough, but to be suppressed, beleaguered, and thwarted at every turn can be overwhelming. These narratives offer some ways to find some peace in the storm that will allow you to recharge, reenergize, ad regain your composure to keep on going.

Take Care of You: Engage in Self Care

The most important part of your journey is you. As Black professionals, we dedicate so much time to our careers, education, family, and friends we forget to take care of ourselves. The authors discuss how to focus on self-care through meditation, creating an environment, or safe space, where you can enjoy peace, confiding in your circle of trusted friends and equals, as well as relying on faith can help you cope with the hostile environment that student affairs can often be, especially for Black people. As mentioned before, Black professionals show up in higher education for the sake of Black students and other students of color, to lead the way through the treacherous ground. If you don't care for yourself and fall prey to the elements surrounding you, who will lead them?

Speak Up!: Remember, You Matter!

In an environment that can seek to squelch Black voices, it is important that Black voices be heard. Not only for the sake of the students and their experience but also for the progression of your career, the inclusion of your ingenuity and innovation, and a place at the decision-making table. Whether it is your individual voice or the collective voice of Black professionals across campus, there is power in using your voice. Like anything else, using your voice comes will consequences. However, remember that, despite the opposition and negative influences, you matter! What you bring to the table matters. How you show up and provide leadership matters. And because you matter, your voice needs to be heard.

Trust Yourself and Know Your Worth

Amid the stress and turmoil that accompanies navigating the terrain of student affairs, Black professionals can get lost. Some of them succumb to the negative environment, letting it affect their sense of belonging and leaving them feeling isolated, overworked, and ineffective. Some work themselves to the bone to prove their worth. Others utilize the tools and coping mechanisms they have collected during their time in the field to bolster them. While faced with many reasons to give up, the experiences shared to encourage other Black professionals to stick to their guns and keep going. They encourage you to know your opponent and develop strategies to keep you aligned with your mission and vision. Knowing your power and listening to your inner voice is also advised to find a place of peace and strength from which to operate.

THEME 3: YOU GON' GET ME: ALL OF ME!

Being Black in predominately White spaces always comes with the temptation to assimilate to attain success. The pressure to shelve your own personality, cultural expression and affinity for your Blackness is real. Black men and women in the student affairs profession pay higher prices for being themselves in predominately White institutions. The authors recount experiences where the construction of their masculinity, the choice to build a family or to just be their authentic selves are called into question. The choices we make as Black professionals, particularly in student affairs, about how we represent ourselves in majority White spaces are often riddled with concern and sometimes fear. These professionals advocate using authenticity to find their power and assert themselves in these spaces. They offer that by using your morals and values as your compass, you should be able to find your way to success.

Don't Get Caught Up: Be Intentional in What You Do

Black men and women in student affairs are viewed through a lens colored with stereotypes, malicious tropes, and misinformation. They are often positioned as loud, overbearing, and threatening. The images of the "angry Black woman" or the dangerous "thug" are often superimposed over the competent, accomplished, and professional practitioners we present in these predominantly White spaces. These authors suggest not getting sucked into the politics and negativity of the environment but instead being intentional about your presence and purpose. White counterparts and even students will doubt your intellect and credibility. It is important to stay grounded in who you are and what you bring to the table to avoid losing yourself. Being intentional has a practical dimension as well. Black student affairs professionals should intentionally make career plans, choose allies, and prioritize their life.

Let the Spirit Be Your Guide

It should come as no surprise that spirituality is mentioned as a life raft on a rocky sea, such as student affairs. Authored talked about spirituality being a cornerstone of Black culture since entering the country. The authors are adamant about holding fast to spirituality to make it through the whirlwind that is student affairs as a Black professional. Daily affirmations are mentioned to remain grounded and deal with the negative energy found in predominantly White spaces. Staying connected to spiritual practices such as meditation, prayer, and affirmations can also help fight fatigue and keep you energized for navigating the hills and valleys of student affairs. Using aspects of spirituality can help you find your center and stay balanced in both your professional and personal lives.

Put It on Blast: Call Out the Injustice

Black student affairs professionals constantly struggle to control their own narratives in predominantly White spaces, at no fault of their own. Many Black professionals feel they are forced to live a double life in these spaces to be effective or advance. Faced with unyielding attacks on their character, professionalism, and image, some professionals might choose to "go along to get along." However, the authors in this text feel that the best way to succeed, not only on the job but personally, is to stay entrenched in being yourself and calling out the negativity and those who bring it to the environment. They advocate for finding the strength to expose the "racial antics" used to undermine the work of Black student affairs professionals. Vocalizing your experience of and sources of inequality in your institution can be a powerful tool for institutional change in your organization. You should find comfort in being who you are, with authenticity, and unapologetically in White spaces regardless of how you think you are being perceived.

ABOUT THE AUTHORS

EDITOR

Antione D. Tomlin, PhD, PCC, is an associate professor and department chair of Academic Literacies at Anne Arundel Community College. He earned his PhD in Language, Literacy and Culture from the University of Maryland, Baltimore County, his MA in Higher Education Administration with a specialization in student affairs from Morgan State University, and his BS in Psychology from Stevenson University. Antione is also an ICF-trained and certified Life Coach.

AUTHORS

Dyrell Ashley is a proud native of the Southside of Chicago. He began his collegiate career at Illinois State University, where he obtained his bachelor's degree in Psychology and Pre- nursing. After working in higher education, Dyrell returned to his Alma Mater to obtain his master's degree in College Student Personnel Administration with a graduate certificate in Women's, Gender, and Sexuality Studies. Mr. Ashley is a current doctoral student at the University of Illinois Urbana-Urbana Champaign, where he is studying Education, Policy, Organization, and Leadership with a focus on Diversity in Education. Dyrell currently serves as the Sr. Diversity Programs Specialist at Constellation Energy. An educator, artist, mentor, advocate, and soon-to-be father, this Gates Millennium Scholar is a committed diversity, equity, and inclusion expert who has committed his talents to the field of making the world a little better one step at a time.

Marcedes Butler, EdD, is a seasoned higher education administrator and expert in helping students graduate. Her publication list includes articles and conference proceedings supporting student retention, persistence, and advisement, particularly on degree completion for nontraditional and at-risk populations. Dr. Butler's most recent book chapter is titled *Who is Going to Mentor Us? Black Women Administrator and Our Leadership Journeys* and her research interests focus on self and collective efficacy, building inclusive learning communities, and appreciative advising. Dr. Butler won the 2022 National Academic Advising Association (NACADA) Region 9 Excellence in Advising—Advising Administrator Certificate of Merit. Additionally, Dr. Butler owns an education consulting business, AcademicHelp101.com, and currently works as the Learning Concierge at the University of Nevada, Las Vegas (UNLV), assisting working adults in earning their college degree entirely online through the workforce development program, MGM International College Opportunity Program (COP).

Eboni Chism MS. Ed, has a Master of Science in Education in the College Student Personnel Administration program from Southern Illinois University-Edwardsville. Eboni is an academic and student success professional, educator, and advocate for the success and mental wellness of nontraditional adult students. She is currently working at Saint Louis University, where she is also pursuing her doctoral degree in Education in the Higher Education program. Eboni considers herself a Black activist builder, healer, and educator. She uses her voice to encourage, motivate, inspire, and uplift. Eboni lives in Illinois with her husband and two sons. When she is not serving in her role as student affairs professional, you can find her screaming on the sidelines of her son's sporting event.

Jamarco "Dr. J" Clark is originally from Pensacola, FL, and moved to Iowa in 2010 to further his academic and athletic career at Iowa Wesleyan University where he obtained a bachelor's degree in Educational Foundation. He holds a master's degree in Strategic Leadership from Mount Mercy University. Jamarco also holds a Doctor of Education in student affairs administration and leadership from the University of Wisconsin La Crosse. Jamarco's research interests are Black male student affairs professional wellbeing and secondary trauma in student affairs professionals. Jamarco serves as the Assistant Dean of Students and Director of Leadership & Engagement at The University of Iowa.

Ebony S. Cole, EdD, has been active in higher education for nine years, primarily as a financial aid administrator, with extended responsibilities that focus on student support and success. Ebony currently serves on multiple institutional committees that participate in programs devoted to providing current and prospective students with strategies to overcome barriers derived from their socioeconomic and intersectional identities to achieve their lifelong goal of obtaining a collegiate degree. In 2021, Ebony earned her Doctor of Education from Northcentral University. In addition to her doctorate, she also holds a Master of Business Administration and a Bachelor of Psychology, which she received from Albertus Magnus College in Connecticut. In addition to her academic success, she is also a licensed cosmetologist and mother of two wonderful young adult children.

Kristina Collier graduated from the University at Buffalo in 2019 with a master's degree in Higher Education Administration. Kristina is currently working on a PhD in Higher Education Administration as well and just rounded out the first year in the doctoral program. Kristina is passionate about social justice, and research interest looks to investigate the relationship between natural hair and higher education and the ideas of White supremacy, anti-Blackness, and marginalization. Kristina currently works full-time in Residential Life and is always looking for ways to use the platform to bring about change in institutions around Social Justice and Inclusion.

Jamie J. Doss, MA, LCPC, is a Licensed Clinical Professional Counselor who has worked in higher education since 2018. She currently serves as a Talent Sourcer at Cornell University and is also a doctoral student at Saint Louis University pursuing a PhD in Higher Education Administration. In addition, she is a mental health provider that has worked in behavioral healthcare for 13 years. Jamie holds a Master of Arts in Counseling from Lindenwood University-Belleville, as well as a Bachelor of Science in Psychology and a Bachelor of Science in Biological Sciences from Southern Illinois University Edwardsville. She is a passionate lifelong learner and member of the higher education and behavioral healthcare communities.

Sarah Holliday, MS, recently transitioned from higher education into the tech industry in 2021. Prior to her career change, Ms. Holliday worked as a higher education administrator for eight years working with non-traditional and traditional-aged students in various areas related to career development, professional development, and personal enrichment. Ms. Holliday's experience extends beyond the administrative role, as she has over a decade of teaching experience in both the private sector and higher education. Sarah has taught various subjects such as Developmental Reading and Writing, English, Career Development, and Business in asynchronous, hybrid, and synchronous formats. Sarah has a Bachelor of Arts from UMBC in English (Communication and Technology), a master's from Walden University in Instructional Design and Technology (Training and Performance Improvement), and is currently pursuing her Doctorate. Sarah is passionate about technology, innovation, and strategic thinking.

Andrew Johnson, EdD, has 20 years of experience as an administrator, coach, educator, and mentor. After working in the field of Health and Physical Education and Athletics for 18 years, he transitioned to doing Diversity, Equity, and Inclusion work. Currently, he is the Director of Multicultural Student Affairs at the University of North Georgia and the owner of Andrew Johnson Consulting, where he works with organizations and schools by providing tools to ensure that all students have an accessible and equitable educational experience. As a first-generation student, he earned his bachelor's degree in Sports Administration from Lock Haven University, followed by a master's degree in Sports Coaching from the United States Sports Academy. Most recently, he earned his doctorate in Higher Education Management from the University of Pittsburgh. Personally, Dr. Johnson is the husband of his college sweetheart Ildiko Benoit-Johnson and the father of three beautiful children, Alaina, Savana, and Ace.

Carl Mackey is an artist, educator, and activist, Carl has worked with students at all levels, and focuses his energies on restorative justice issues such as access and closing achievement gaps, highlighting issues of diversity, inclusion, and equity in educational spaces. As an activist and champion of LGBTQA issues, he has been involved in queer youth development, HIV prevention education, and mental health issues for Queer people of color for over two decades. As a certified peer counselor, he facilitated the men's groups Harambe Jahard and Imani Umoja for the Illinois Cook County Health Department. He served as the president of OutEd, an organization for Queer graduate students in Education at the University of Pennsylvania. Carl earned a Bachelor of Science with majors in Computer Science and Sociology from Northeastern Illinois University, a Master of Science in Education focusing on Higher Education Management from the University of Pennsylvania, and is currently working on his PhD in School Psychology at Stephen F. Austin State University.

Erica McBride, MSW, is a St. Louis, MO native. She attended Saint Louis Public schools for my K–12 education, followed by attending Truman State University. At Truman State, she received a Bachelor of Science degree in Health Science, became a member of Delta Sigma Theta Sorority Inc, and a McNair Scholar. After graduating, she became a case manager within a nonprofit for people with developmental disabilities. Within this organization, she created and became president of the diversity, equity and inclusion committee. In 2020, she obtained her master's in social work. Two months prior to graduation she became the program coordinator in the department of biology within a predominantly White institution. During this role, she developed and implemented programs to recruit and retain students from diverse backgrounds. She currently works within the Cross-Cultural Center, as a Program Coordinator II who facilitates the MLK Scholars and Safe Zone Competency program, which strives to shed light on the systemic use of heteronormativity and cis-normativity on campus. She has facilitated and presented on several topics pertaining to diversity, equity, and inclusion within higher education. She is currently a PhD student within the Higher Education Administration program at Saint Louis University.

Katina Moten, EdD, has worked in higher education for over 20 years. She started her professional journey holding positions at the Penn State College of Medicine in Hershey, PA, and at Franklin & Marshall College in Lancaster, PA. For the past 16 years, Katina has worked at Penn State University serving as an academic advisor, advancing to director of advising, and then becoming director of academic support & advising services. She now serves as the inaugural director of Engineering Connect, a program that aims to improve the persistence of first-year, preengineering students at Penn State's 20 undergraduate campuses. Katina graduated with an EdD in higher education administration from Immaculata University. Prior to completing her doctoral degree, she received her MA in leadership and liberal studies from Duquesne University and earned a BA in biology from Bloomsburg University. Katina currently resides in Harrisburg, PA., serving her community through her involvement in Zeta Phi Beta Sorority, Inc.

Michelle A. Nelson, is an equity advocate, education researcher, and higher education professional. She is a Detroit, MI native with more than 18 years working both in academic and student affairs serving in various roles such as Assistant Provost of Student and Global Affairs, Assistant Director of Student Success, Director of International Education as well as an Academic and Career advisor. Also, she has taught as an adjunct faculty giving her the ability and insight to serve students holistically both in and outside the classroom. She holds a liberal arts degree in Political Science and French, an MBA in Strategic Management, and a PhD in Educational Leadership. Her research explores relevant issues focused on sense of belonging, identity development, social justice education, and global education that promote transformative learning experiences, especially for students of color. In addition to her work commitments, she enjoys traveling, which includes over 30 countries, 37 states, and quality time with her family.

Caryn Reed-Hendon, PhD, is the Founding Director of Diversity, Equity & Inclusion at Lawrence Technological University. At LTU, she is responsible for the daily operations for the Office for Diversity, Equity & Inclusion, and also works in support of the President, the Board of Trustees, the Dean of Students, and University Human Resources. She has 20 years of higher education experience, specifically in the area of student affairs, with a focus on mentorship, pipeline programs, and JEDI professional development. She has served in leadership for a number of professional and educational committees and has worked collaboratively to present materials at regional, national, and international conferences. Dr. Reed-Hendon's memberships include Sigma Gamma Rho Sorority, Inc., National Association of Minority Medical Educators, National Association of Diversity Officers in Higher Education, Queens Collective, International Leaderships Association, King Chavez Parks Future Faculty Fellows, and NASPA: Student Affairs Administrators in Higher Education.

Nathan A. Stephens, PhD, is an Assistant Professor in Social Work at Illinois State University. He completed his Bachelor of Social Work at Columbia College, his Master of Social Work, and a PhD in Educational Leadership and Policy Analysis at the University of Missouri-Columbia. Dr. Stephens is certified as a social justice educator through the Social Justice Training Institute and has over 15 years of experience doing trainings and presentations that focus on equity, diversity, inclusion, and social justice. Past audiences include professional conferences, legislative bodies, police departments, corporations, student organizations, academic units, campus leadership, and athletic departments to name a few. Prior to teaching full time, he worked in student affairs for over 14 years in diversity and social justice-related spaces. Dr. Stephens' research examines ecological systems and their impact on Black boys and men, through the lenses of racialization, racism, complex stress/trauma, equity, and justice.

Dana G. Stilley, PhD, is dedicated to advocating for equity, social justice, educational attainment, and leadership development. Dr. Stilley earned a BS degree from Brown University, an MBA from the Columbia Graduate School of Business, and a PhD from Old Dominion University. Following a successful career on Wall Street, Dana began work in higher education. Currently, Dr. Stilley is an adjunct instructor of Mathematics, and the founder and CEO of The Stilley Agency, which specializes in dissertation coaching and editing. Dr. Stilley is a valued leader throughout her community. She serves as a Board Member for several nonprofits, and is the President of her local Board of Education. Additionally, she is a member of Delta Sigma Theta Sorority, Inc. Dr. Stilley has been honored for her outstanding leadership, mentorship, and scholarship. She continues to focus on sharing the experiences of African American women in leadership. Dana is married to Derrick Stilley and they have one son.

Terrell L. Strayhorn, PhD, is a Professor of Higher Education and Women's, Gender, & Sexuality Studies at Illinois State University, where he also directs the Higher Ed PhD program. Previously, he served as Provost and Senior Vice President of Academic Affairs at Virginia Union University (VUU), where he continues as Visiting Scholar in the VUU School of Education and Director of the Center for the Study of Historically Black Colleges and Universities (HBCUs). One of the world's leading experts on racial equity, student success, and sense of belonging in learning and workplaces, Strayhorn is author of 11 books and over 200 peer-reviewed journal articles, chapters, and influential reports. He is Specialty Chief Editor of *Frontiers in Education* (Higher Ed), Guest Editor of *Youth and Sustainability*; Diversity Scholar-in-Residence at Harrisburg Area College, and member of the Children's Defense Fund Freedom Schools Research Advisory Board and Alpha Phi Alpha Fraternity, Incorporated.

Tasha Wilson serves as a Case Manager in the Office of Inclusion & Institutional Equity at Towson University. She received a bachelor's degree in Human Ecology from the University of Maryland Eastern Shore, a master's degree in Education from Towson University, and a master's degree in Social Work from Morgan State University. Currently, she is obtaining a doctoral degree in Christian Leadership: Ministry Leadership from Liberty University. She serves as the Research & Scholarship Chair for ACPA Coalition for Multicultural Affairs Directorate Board, Speakers Bureau member for RAINN (Rape, Abuse & Incest National Network), and Communications Chair for TU's Black Faculty & Staff Association. Outside her role in Student Affairs, Tasha is an International Best-Selling Author, Speaker, and Entrepreneur. Her zeal is in empowering millennial women to get unstuck by mastering the inner critic to authentically live a fulfilling life. She has spoken across the United States, New Zealand, and Australia.

Made in the USA
Middletown, DE
15 September 2023

38588210R00084